Hisne

The Jewish Struggle in Kurdistan

Yitzchak Baruch

Hisne
The Jewish Struggle in Kurdistan

Senior Editors & Producers: ContentNow

Translation : Darya Ram
Cover Illustration: Avi Mazor
Design : Moran Konfino

Copyright © 2016 by
Yitzhak Baruch

All rights reserved. No part of this book may be translated, reproduced, stored in a retrieval system or transmitted, in any form or by any means, electronic, photocopying, recording or otherwise, without prior permission in writing from the author and publisher.

ISBN: 9 789655 505641

Sole International distributor:
ContentoNow
3 Habarzel St. 6971007 Tel-Aviv, Israel
netanel@contentonow.com
www.ContentoNow.com

Dedicated to my wife and closest friend, Rinat and my children, Dana, Shirley, Shai and Nir

It was a house of mourning, though few tears were shed there. I sat next to my Aunt Hisne, then 84 years old. I held her hand and listened to her words. "Two days ago we had a short circuit at home," she told me, sighing. "I called Yehoshua, my youngest son. He lives not far from us. He came in, fixed it and went home. Not even an hour had passed before I came into the kitchen to find my husband lying on the floor, his face drooping all the way from the left side of his chin to his right eye. It was a severe stroke - there was no way he could survive it. He had no chance..."

Oh, Gribo, I mumbled to myself. Gribo...
Hisne went on with her story, but I was no longer paying attention. My thoughts sailed far away, back to all the stories she told me as a child. My thoughts turned to far away Kurdistan, to the high, snowy mountains, to poverty and suffering. I was thinking of Hisne and Grib's early life together in the Jewish courts of Baghdad. I'm not sure why, but I always felt like I was the only one to whom she ever told these stories.
It's interesting, I thought. After all, she does have children of her own. True, there were seven and only five are left, but still - every time I visited her, she opened her heart to me. The stories she told me were the kind of stories you tell only the people closest to you, or a confidant, and I was only her nephew, as old as her youngest child. I belonged to a different generation, a different country, a different mentality, and yet...
"Isn't that so?" Hisne suddenly asked.
"Isn't what...?" I replied, embarrassed. It was like I wasn't there at all during those few moments. I glanced around to see whether anyone had taken notice. Luckily, they were all engrossed in conversation with one another; no one had even looked my way.
"No matter," she said. "That's just how it goes. He died at a ripe old age."

"That's true," I replied.

I sat in the crowded room for two more hours, listening to the loud conversations around me. Hisne continued talking and talking, but no longer to me - instead she conversed with my sister Simha, who sat on her other side.

Perhaps you have also had this feeling about someone close to you, someone who seems as if they will escape death, one of those people for whom everything passes by. A person who is never surprised, never excited and never wonders - the kind of person who never takes anything too seriously. Such was Gribo, or Grib.

Every time fighting broke out or an argument was heard in the house, even just a minor disagreement or an annoying question, Gribo would dismiss it, throw his hands in the air and let out a long sigh. With his sharp voice he would say, "Ahh, shukloh", meaning: let it go, and quickly add, "It's all nonsense anyhow."

In truth, I must admit that even as a child I was always happy to have Gribo around. In him I saw a man who always brought everyone back to sanity, and back to reality. He is the one who always managed to ground us – the one I always wanted to be near: like a compass and a strong and sturdy anchor for us to hold on to.

Whenever a crisis occurred, Gribo was the one to calm everyone down, to make arrangements, to pick up groceries from the market or from the shop, to take care of everything and return everyone to solid ground, as if he was saying...Guys, life goes on.

At least that was the case until the day I saw him break down for the first time in my life: it was six years ago, when he lost his son, Naji. I saw him at the funeral, standing over the open grave, sobbing loudly with tears flooding his eyes.

"Naji," he called, "Naaaajiiiii..."

We had to hold on to him to stop him from collapsing. No, not you Gribo, my heart cried. You're the one that should be keeping us grounded, you're the anchor. A great gush of tears washed my face. I wiped my eyes and covered them with dark sunglasses. Gribo, the strong and marvelous man, now needed the support of his two sons - for otherwise he would have collapsed right on the ground, shattering into pieces.

It seems that every man has his own threshold for suffering. Gribo had one too. I saw him deal with loss more than once: when his brothers passed away, one after the other, and when my father, Shmuel, his best friend and brother-in-law passed away. Shmuel "Shamca", was Hisne's brother. I saw him when his daughter Rachel passed away at 15 from cancer, 35 years earlier. Gribo always kept a straight face and restrained himself. He was realistic; he always looked forward, into the future. Yet here, today, above his son's grave...

Perhaps it's his old age, I pondered. Gribo is not a young man - 75 this year. Perhaps he was feeling weak or tired. Gribo faded away that day. He lost all will to live. In the following six years he grew weaker and weaker, lost his self confidence and his joie de vivre.

About two weeks before he died, I watched him cross the busy intersection across the road from the Israeli Television Building in Romema, Jerusalem. He crossed the street diagonally, perched over his walking cane, slowly making his way with heavy, stumbling steps. I stopped my car and waited for him to cross. I saw him from behind; he didn't even notice me there. He was dragging himself, bent over his cane, in the busiest spot in town, as if he was saying, "Enough, I can't stand life anymore".

I sat in the house of mourning for over two hours. I spoke very little, mostly allowing my thoughts to wander away to places that even the wildest imagination wouldn't believe. When I got up to leave, I saw black spots around me. I was unsteady. My wife held on to me. "Are you alright?" she asked.

"Yes, I must have gotten up too quickly," I replied, knowing full well the real reason. I started making my way toward the exit. Before I left, I went into Gribo's room. I stared at the photos hanging on the wall - images of his children, Rachel and Naji, who had passed away, and images of himself. It felt like a farewell ceremony from this dear man.

Our family had come to Israel from Kurdistan. Even as a child I always wondered how we got there of all places, and why we had to leave. I never ceased questioning my family about it, especially my mother and my Aunt Hisne.

Her stories sailed back in the past, to days no one else could remember.
"Read the Torah, my son," she would tell me.
"Does the Torah have a chapter about our family?" I wondered aloud, childishly.
Hisne didn't answer. She smiled secretively. After a very long silence she would hint, "Yes, the Torah is all about us. It says we arrived there a long, long time ago..."
Even when I grew up and understood what she meant, I never stopped looking for my family's sources and for the origins of the Kurdistan Jewry. One bible verse in particular was engraved in my memory. It is a verse from the Book of Kings that in my mind always seemed like it was describing my family's history. I read it to Hisne time and again. She always listened attentively and smiled.
"The King of Assyria deported Israel to Assyria and settled them in Halah, in Gozan on the Khabur River and in towns of the Medes" (2 Kings 18:11). This was my own family's exile, and the first exile of the people of Israel. It really did take place "a long time ago," as my Aunt Hisne had said - in 733 BC.
At that time, Tiglath-Pileser III ruled over Assyria. He widened his reign to extend all the way from Egypt to Turkey. His was a system of conquest, annexation and exile, a system that soon became a distinct symbol of the Assyrian occupation. The Assyrians exiled every population that recognized their authority but dared to rebel. I read this verse again and again, each time understanding it better, for this exile was the destiny of my family. Until her very last day on earth, my mother

told us that "Tulan resh havora," meaning: We sat on the Khabur River. That's where the Kurdistan exile began. All that was left in the land of Israel was the Judean Kingdom, which held to its status as an independent state for 125 years. Many changes came over the Middle East. Empires came and went, and the Assyrians fell and were replaced by the Babylonians. The Babylonians also went on a conquest tour around the Middle East, and in 597 B.C., Nebuchadnezzar went to war in the land of Israel. He conquered the entirety of Jerusalem, capital of the Judean Kingdom, and forced exile over King Jeconiah. "He carried all Jerusalem into exile: all the officers and fighting men, and all the skilled workers and artisans" (2 Kings 24:14). He was replaced as ruler by Zedekiah. This was the classic method of exiling the leadership and the essential professionals and placing in their stead a new king, a Babylonian subject, who increased the taxes paid to the King of Babylon. In 586 B.C. Nebuchadnezzar came to Jerusalem a second time. He conquered it, destroyed the Holy Temple and exiled the remaining Judeans to Babylon.

Following these exiles, a large community of Jews was established in Babylon and Assyria. The Jewish settlement in Babylon grew, and many Jewish refugees arrived, mostly following the destruction of the Second Temple.

Towns with a Jewish majority arose, such as Nehardea and Nusaybin. There, the Jewish inhabitants were able to nurture their nationality even more so than their brothers in the land of Israel, whose communities grew thinner during and following the days of the Bar Kokhba revolt.

The Jewish "kibbutz" developed its own folklore and lifestyle. The kibbutz maintained contact with Jerusalem using pilgrim convoys which left various Babylonian cities and passed through Nusaybin on their way to the land of Israel. One of the most famous personalities to have traveled that path in those times was Hillel the Elder, who subsequently made his home in the land of Israel and became head of the Sanhedrin during the Second Temple period.

From reading books and hearing stories we know of the Eastern European Jewish towns, we know of the Golden Age of Spanish Jewry, we know of Yemenite Jewry and other communities around the world. But regarding that first exile, dubbed the "Exile of the Ten Lost Tribes", hardly anything has been written. For that reason, very little was known about them, and even less was known about their lifestyle, their community, their culture, their relationships with their gentile neighbors and so on.

What is known is that they were exiled to somewhere near the Khabur River and Tell Halaf, in the mountains of modern-day Kurdistan. They were not people of books, but of work - laborers, which is why they didn't write an account of their exile. Their primary goal was to survive in a country that was difficult in terms of topography, climate and demography. Their Muslim neighbors made life even harder. The few testimonies we have of that exile came from travelers who found themselves in the area, and made a note of it in their diaries.

The Assyrian exile began in 722 B.C. During the first few hundred years, Jewish communities existed both in mixed towns and in Jewish quarters. In mixed towns such as Akra, Zakho, Amadiya, Al-Qamishli and Nusaybin, Jews lived alongside Christians and Muslims. Jews also lived in rural settlements, such as Harran and Barzan. In many places, primarily in mountainous regions, Jews sometimes lived in caves, "shkafte" in Aramaic.

The Jewish community in Kurdistan continued to exist through the centuries, though it was disconnected from other Jewish centers - even those which were nearby, such as Babylon, in modern day Iraq. The rugged mountainous topography made it very difficult to travel, and weather was similarly a problem. In addition, highway robbers were common in valleys and mountain passes, and they posed a serious risk that discouraged free movement in the area.

Barzan was considered one of the most important Jewish settlements. Jews would say: "From Sindur (a city in Kurdistan) the Torah will come, and the word of God from Barzan."

The Jewish traveler, Rabbi Benjamin of Tudela, who visited the area in 1170 A.D., wrote: "They come from the first exile of King Shalmaneser, and they speak Aramaic." At the time of his visit, a messianic revival took place in Kurdistan which left its mark among the Jews. It was instigated by David Alroy, who held a national and messianic vision. The Jews spoke Aramaic, which was similar to the Babylonian Talmud and to the Targum Onkelos translation of the Torah. Their Christian-Assyrian neighbors spoke it as well.

One famous name in Kurdistan Jewry was Asenath Barzani, a woman who headed a yeshiva during the 17th century. She was the daughter of Rabbi Samuel Barzani, who established a yeshiva in Kurdistan. Asenath married her father's greatest student, Rabbi Jacob Mizrahi, who inherited his teacher's place as head of the yeshiva while Asenath taught there. After the death of Jacob she headed the yeshiva herself, until her death in 1670.

Asenath Barzani wrote commentary for the Book of Proverbs, but sadly it was lost. The respect and adoration held for her by her peers can be gleaned from a letter she received from Rabbi Pinhas Hariri, in which he referred to her as the "teacher of teachers".

According to scholars Raziel Memet and Avi Blair, Jewish life in Kurdistan was lawless. Robbery, murder and rape were common and the Jewry's disconnect from the enlightened, free world and from the rest of the Jewish communities meant that no one would come to their aid.

In 1848, Jewish traveler J. J. Benjamin visited Kurdistan. He wrote of the damage done to the Jews by the Kurds:. In his own words, "They eat their bread by the sweat of their brow, often dipped in their own heart's blood." He emphasized that the Jewish women who went to the tahara mikvah were particularly vulnerable; many were tortured and sometimes murdered.

One well-known story in Kurdistan told of a Jewish woman who went to dip in the water spring. Three Muslim men passing by, or who perhaps were stalking her, as my Aunt Hisne suggests - wanted to have their way with her. The woman grabbed a thick tree branch and hit one of them in the head. He fell and died instantly. The other two then murdered her in cold blood.

Another story is told about Yehuda Barzan, born in 1865, who immigrated to Jerusalem. He was forced to flee his country, Kurdistan, after watching a member of the Kurdish leader family Barzani torture and murder a Jewish girl. He avenged her and subsequently made aliyah to Israel, fearing retribution. All of this is known thanks to testimony from his son, Jacob, though locals could never imagine that a Jewish man would do such a thing.

Jacob Barzan was one of the founders of Yesud HaMa'ala, a member of Hashomer and the Haganah, and one of the founders of Kfar Yona. His son, Zvi Bar, was a commander of the Israeli Border Police and Mayor of Ramat Gan.

Jewish literature further mentions Jews who traveled from Kurdistan to Israel as early as the 18th century, and settled in Safed. Kurdistani Jews were also among the first of the Eastern Jewry to settle in Jerusalem. Initial immigration was slow, but soon the stream grew, as the constant persecutions increased the rate of departure. Yehuda Barzan, who fled to Jerusalem from Kurdistan, is only one name in a long list.

Our story begins in Barzan, a small town in Iraqi Kurdistan. Up until the end of World War I, approximately 400 Jews lived in and around the town. It was a religious community, which included rabbis, shohets (ritual animal slaughterers), mohels, cantors and other religious professionals.

Although the majority of community members were illiterate, they enjoyed a full Jewish lifestyle. For instance, every Friday afternoon before the Sabbath, they surrounded the town with wires marking a 'Sabbath zone'. Additionally, they marked grassy and weedy areas, fearing that walking through them might crush the plants, causing a desecration of the Sabbath. Holidays were celebrated in three or four places. Each extended family had at least one member who could read and perform the holiday rituals, so families who lived near Barzan would often come together to celebrate.

This was the situation up until the end of World War I. In the post-war years, between 1919 and 1922, waves of rebellion arose against the British. Jews ran away to Akra and nearby villages. Barzan slowly emptied of its Jewish residents, and by 1947 only 20 Jews remained. They too came to Israel a few years later: in 1950 and 1951.

The borders separating Iran, Iraq, Syria, Turkey and the former USSR created an impossible environment for the Kurds. Their centuries-long dream of independence was never fulfilled in any of these countries. The promises made to them while under the reign of the British Empire were not kept, nor was the failed intervention by the United Nations helpful. Furthermore, every time their voice was heard in one of the countries in which they resided, it was forcefully silenced.

Well-remembered are the bloody wars between the Turkish Kurds, led by Abdullah Öcalan, and the Turkish

regime. Iraq went one step further, slaughtering Iraqi Kurds any time they would raise their heads, even beyond the Irani border.

During the 1950s, '60s and early '70s, Mustafa Barzani of the Barzan village led the Iraqi Kurds in an armed rebellion against the Iraqi authorities, demanding autonomy. For four decades the Iraqi government fought the Kurds' right to autonomy, even as regimes replaced one another. The cruelest of them all was Iraq's last ruler, Saddam Hussein. He spared no methods, including gassing civilians as he did in Halabja.

Beyond the towns and villages were also small mountainous settlements, such as Barzan, which were built near caves. That area has many caves and locals built their homes near the entrances. The cave became a part of the home - a storage room or a place to hide when the bombs fell. Houses were usually one-story high, with the exception of a few houses which had attics. They were built of clay bricks, while the synagogues were built of large ashlar stones.

No paved roads connected these settlements, so no vehicles traveled between them. Distance was measured by the number of days it took to walk from one village to another, or number of days riding a donkey - for those who could afford one. Nor were the settlements integrated. Separate villages often had variations in language and pronunciation, even if they were relatively near each other and only a few day's walk.

Regardless, meetings still took place, mostly about commerce centered on wheat, rice, wool, fabric and animals. These meetings were also an opportunity to pass along information about the political state of the community, about relationships with neighbors, and of course gossip: who died and who is living, who married whom, who fought whom, and so on.

"Like any good Jewish community, fights would often begin in Temple on the Sabbath," my mother used to tell me. "One time a heated debate broke out between Moshe Gabai, head of the Jewish community in Zakho, and Sabto Zaken, my grandfather - my mother's father. Like many other disputes, this one started from some nonsense everyone soon forgot. It quickly turned into loud yelling, mutual slanders and curses that I hesitate to repeat.

In the midst of arguing, with his face red with fury and beads of sweat on his brow, Sabto Zaken stood up on a bench and cried at Moshe Gabai: 'You will not have a say here! Tomorrow I'll go fetch a new cantor from Dohuk.' He left temple with his sons following him. The next day he took his stick and his bag and marched towards Dohuk, three days south of Zakho."

Life in Barzan was led in the shadow of the Kurdish rebellion. The year was 1922, and Kurdish acts of rebellion against the British was underway. The British decided to retaliate by bombing Barzan, home of the rebellion leader Mahmud Barzani and his five sons, most famously Mustafa Barzani.

The bombing was horrific. Loud explosions traumatized the entire area. In the midst of all the noise and commotion, the voice of Mualem Zacharya was suddenly heard above the crowd: 'Take the children, don't forget the children... everyone run inside the temple...'

His booming voice intermingled with the screams of the women and the crying of the children. Everyone ran in a frenzy towards the temple, which was located in the center of the village next to the entrance of a wide cave; it was made of large black ashlar stones. Inside the cave were many small crypts, like tiny rooms. Everyone ran inside: Jews, Muslims, and Christians.

Pieces of clay from the walls flew in every direction; shrapnel and soil filled the air. It was a living hell.

'Is everyone here?' echoed the voice of Mualem Zacharya as he stepped into the cave. 'The ones who aren't here

must be in the small cave,' answered one of the men. Many of the children were barefoot, as were some of the mothers. And most of those mothers were children themselves: fourteen, fifteen, and sixteen-year-old girls who still needed their own parents' protection.

The echoing cries of the children made a horrific sound. Sometimes it seemed that it was louder than the sound of the outside explosions. The young mothers were not able to quiet their children, so the older ones tried to calm them down. Suddenly, as if by magic, everything went silent and the children stopped wailing.

'Don't leave yet,' ordered Mualem Zacharya.

A muffled sound from the back of the cave led Mualem Zacharya toward an eighteen-year-old girl carrying her newborn daughter. It was Zere. Her wet, green eyes shone in the darkness of the cave, and her long brown hair, usually tied and covered with a keffiyeh, had fallen loose and was draped about her shoulders. Her bare feet poked out from under her long brown dress, which was tied at the waist with a red scarf.

'Where is your husband?' asked Mualem Zacharya.

'My husband?" she cried, 'You know very well where my husband is! You married me at thirteen-years-old. What was the rush? I cannot bear this burden any longer! I buried both my sons with my own hands. I washed and cleansed them, dug their graves... and food? I gather it from the Muslims, one handful at a time: wheat, rice, flour, semolina. I pick vegetables in the mountains. My husband eats it all - he gets up at night, finds whatever food I've managed to gather, and eats it!'

'Silence, woman!' Mualem Zacharya scolded, giving her a look that hinted this was not the time or place to be discussing these matters. 'Kula min ulha,' he said, 'Everything is from God. There is a war. Now cover your hair.'

'And when will this war end?' asked Zere, putting her daughter down, straightening her hair, and tightening

the Keffiyeh in circles around her head.
'What is going to happen to us? When will it end?' joined the others in the cave, coming together around Mualem Zacharya. 'Only ten years ago the Turks fought the Persians, again making Kurds the buffer. That passed, but now we're being bombed again. When will it end?'
'Times have changed, ya jamaa, times have changed,' Mualem Zacharya replied solemnly. 'The Ottoman Empire collapsed and the young officers' coup overthrew the sultan. Today they're building a new Turkey and looking towards the west. They no longer want control over the entire area. They want a Turkey for the Turkish only, a Turkey clean of any other nationals.'
Everyone listened attentively to his words. Mualem Zacharya had great influence over the town's Jewry. He was the rabbi, the sage, the mohel, the shohet - and was considered the authority.
'We Kurds present a problem to them,' he added. 'They want to show the world there is no Kurdish problem in their country - so they've decided to eliminate us. Surely you remember how they executed Abd el-Salam ten years ago. Today we're dealing with the British. They've taken the country over from the Turks and promised they'll give the Kurds a state of our own. When it became clear that they have no intention of keeping that promise, the Kurds began a rebellion. I believe we will have independence one day and peace will return, letting us finally live like we did in the old days, every man under his vine and under his fig tree, as the bible says.'
'Inshallah,' the crowd replied quietly, 'God willing.'
One by one they began to leave the cave and return to their homes, or what was left of them.
Once again they had to take care of the wounded, calm down the anxious, and quickly rebuild - before the harsh winter arrived and covered the area with a thick blanket of snow. They had to gather and store food and create

a place in the cave that would be warm enough to live in - to rekindle the fire of life.
For that they needed to gather firewood, work that usually occupied most of the children's waking hours. The poor little ones carried heavy parcels of wood on their backs all the way from the fields, forests or groves – walking many kilometers a day. The more wood they could bring home, the better chance they had to survive the winter. The fire would burn constantly, day and night, for without it, existence was simply impossible. Lighting the fire posed a problem as well. Not just anyone could do it. Matches were yet to arrive in the distant mountains of Kurdistan, so fires were lit using the age-old technique of rotating a thin wooden bar over another piece of wood, or by grinding two rocks together. Once a fire was burning, it was necessary to keep it alive and add more and more wood to make sure it burned continually. Life in the cave or the home took place around the fire. In the mornings, the children's milk and semolina would be cooked above it and water would be heated for tea. Later in the day, bread was baked on the "saj". Once the adults left for work, the fire was used for boiling water, washing clothes, bathing and cooking. During the night it provided protection from the cold and kept animals from wandering in from the snowy mountains.
The origins of the Kurdish rebellion are rooted in 1919 with the failure to fulfill the provisions of the Treaty of Sèvres. Upon the ending of the First World War, the Paris Peace Conference called for the establishment of the state of Kurdistan, a fact that remained only on paper. During 1922, the British who ruled Iraq acknowledged it as a sovereign state and gave the Kurds the right to self-govern, as part of the new kingdom. The Kurds refused the offer and began fighting for their rights. The rebellion started at Sulaymaniyah. Only in 1924 did the Baghdad government manage to take control

of the Sulaymaniyah area.

Barzan was almost entirely wiped out. Suddenly the demand for caves increased. Almost all of the houses were in ruin. Those that were left standing could no longer provide a decent shelter from bombings. Only the great synagogue, which was built on a cave from large basalt blocks, survived. It felt like no canon in the world could take it down - due to its size and to its holiness.

By the end of World War I, Barzan was home to some 400 Jews. Between 1919 and 1922, following the rebellion against the British, Jews ran away to Akra and nearby villages and only five or six families remained in Barzan. The winter of 1923 was particularly difficult. Some managed to restore the little that was left of their houses using rocks and wood, or goat skin sheets and blankets. Those who failed went inside the caves to live. There were plenty of caves and enough room for all. The most sought-after resource during those cold days was wood for the fire.

Snow covered every part of the earth. No flora survived in the area. That also meant that no food was available. Those who collected or preserved food managed to survive the harsh winter. Those who could afford it bought food in nearby Muslim villages. The most vulnerable of all were the infants.

As shocking as it may sound, winter took its toll among the young ones, who died of starvation or exposure to the cold. This was a simple life, and these deaths were almost accepted without a word. When calculating the natural birth rate and death rate in Kurdistan at that time, we now know that population growth was very small, primarily due to infant mortality.

Due to the difficult topography and climate and the lack of hygiene and proper medical care, the death rate among babies neared 50%. In other words, if a woman had given birth to ten babies in her lifetime, there's a good chance only five of them managed to survive

winter, hunger and disease.
The brutal winter caught Zere and David penniless. Zere's earlier experiences made her fearful of losing her newborn daughter, Hisne.
One day, in the middle of winter, a rumor broke out in the village that aid had arrived and that someone was giving away blankets and bags of flour. All the women immediately began running towards the distributors.
No one remembers who it was that gave the packages away: the British army or the Turkish, perhaps the Iraqis or the Russians. No one knew. When the event was later discussed, a different army was given credit. Regardless, the cold and hungry residents were given five kilograms of blankets and flour each.
David and Zere were among the recipients, with Zere carrying little Hisne in her arms. At the distribution point, everyone was crowding and pushing, each grasping for the much needed and incredibly expensive package. Zere placed Hisne on the snow and began making her way through the commotion and towards the soldiers. When she managed to secure a blanket, she grabbed it and ran towards the cave. David ran after her, holding a bag of flour.
'Thank God,' they cried, 'we're saved!'
Back in their little room in the cave, Zere spread out their new treasures: the blanket and the bag of flour. As she wiped tears from her eyes, neighbors burst in. 'What have you done?' they asked. 'For a bag of flour and a blanket you threw away your child? The whole village can hear her crying!'
"I had a loud voice," Hisne told me many years later.
"Had?" I asked with a smile.
"You laugh," she replied, "but everyone says I shout when I talk."
Hisne and her sisters used to talk in shouts. I remember that when my parents and I paid them a visit, Hisne would ask her daughter Kochava to "Make Uncle Shmuel

a cup of tea". The windows would ring from her loud and sharp voice.

"Laugh all you want," she said with a smile, and continued with her story.

"My father immediately ran from the cave to pick me up. To be honest, I was probably meant to die that very day, a common occurrence."

I listened closely.

"Being so cold and so hungry can make you forget anything - even your own children," she added.

After they survived that winter, better days came to Barzan. The war died down. They were able rebuild the houses, and agriculture flourished. The men and women felt relief, and were possibly on the verge of economic prosperity.

Zere gave birth to two more children: a son named Shmuel, my own father, and a daughter named Sarah. From the moment he was born until his last day on earth, everyone called my father, "Shamca". Hisne was one-and-a-half-years older than Shamca, who himself was one-and-a-half-years older than Sarah. Hisne was born in the winter of 1923, possibly at the end of 1922. Shamca was born in 1924 and Sarah in 1925.
That was the year the League of Nations Border Committee recommended that the Mosul district be annexed to Iraq, and that the Kurdish language be officially recognized. The committee further recommended that Kurdish officials should represent the government in Kurdish territories. When autonomy failed to take hold, an armed rebellion broke out in 1927. This rebellion was more like guerrilla warfare. There was no army that brandished weapons in a war against another army. Instead, the rebellion took the form of localized actions such as surprise attacks on Iraqi military posts, mountain ambushes, sniper fire directed at military convoys, and so on. This type of fighting took a heavy toll on the Iraqi army.
Solitary Kurdish fighters would often take down entire platoons of Iraqi soldiers, marching down the narrow passes of the Kurdistan mountains. The Kurdish soldiers knew this tough mountainous topography well, and they would simply sit and wait. When the Iraqi soldiers were in close range, they would be taken down with machine gun fire.
This nature of fighting hardly affected life in Barzan, for the war took place far from there. It arrived at their

doorstep sporadically, only when the Iraqi army decided to bomb the town following Kurdish action, and despite the fact that Mustafa Barzani had lived there. Generally speaking, the people of Barzan led a normal life - as normal as it could be. This manifested primarily in their agricultural and industrial work.

Grandpa David worked in textiles. He weaved a particular style of trousers that was popular in the area, and he sold them: sometimes for cash and sometimes for food supplies such as rice, flour, oil or beans. Grandma Zere worked as a washerwoman in the houses of the rich, or filtered beans. In her spare time she spun yarn from the wool they bought or were given by the Muslims in exchange for work. The spun yarn was meant for the trousers that grandpa made.

There was not much of a livelihood to be earned from these tasks, yet help was received from the neighbors, as well as the couple's close relationship with the Mullah Mustafa Barzani. A great friendship existed between my grandfather and the Mullah. It was aided by Barzani's affection for the Jews. He saw them as far more loyal than the Arabs, and believed they would never turn their backs on him.

His friendship with David was expressed in games they played together. David was thin and short. He was known as the fastest runner in the region. Barzani loved to compete with him. The competition included more than just running skills: they each had to run from a starting point to an ending point, and back. At the ending point they had to grab an object, such as a knife, a sword, or even some fruit and return.

While running, they were allowed to lean in with their shoulders in an attempt to block their rival. David never won any of these contests. He always knew when to fall or slow down so he wouldn't - God forbid - defeat Barzani.

Barzani would start laughing. 'What happened, David?

You're supposed to be the fastest of them all!'

'Yes,' replied my grandfather. 'But you're faster and stronger...you are the only one I cannot beat.'

Another favorite game for Barzani was egg-breaking. Each man chose an egg that he thought had the strongest shell and tapped the eggs one on the other; the winner was the man who managed to break his fellow's egg.

Here too, David knew to choose an egg with a softer, or even cracked, shell - whatever it took to make sure he wouldn't win over Barzani. The latter would laugh, and David would declare, 'You're good, you're very good... you can't be beat.'

Barzan is surrounded by mountainous scenery, full of water springs and brooks. The region's climate allows for versatile flora almost year-round, apart from the tough winters. Those who knew the different varieties of plants and knew which were edible and which poisonous, would never starve. The high death rate of babies and infants in Barzan and Kurdistan as a whole was partly due to hunger, but mostly due to lack of the most basic antibiotic medication. Children died of influenza, rubella, jaundice and other relatively basic diseases.

Not all the fields were wild fields. There were also vineyards and orchards which belonged to farmers who sold their produce for money or other goods such as clothes, food and animals.

Moshe, David's brother, was one of those land owners. He had both vineyards and orchards, and in relationship to the circumstances in those days, was considered very wealthy. His relationship with Mustafa Barzani was even closer than my grandfather's. He was a highly respected man, both for his riches and for his wisdom. Moshe inherited his riches from his father Baruch, whom the Muslims called Barkuna. The vineyards and orchards that belonged to Baruch were handled by the Muslims who worked for him. This angered the Muslims very much - that a Jewish man owned property and employed them. How is it possible, religiously speaking, that the Jews could outrank the Muslims? According to Islam, it is the superior religion. In Arabic they say, "Al Islam Aalah Va La Yoel a lay..", meaning: Islam is the highest and none can rise above it. This saying is considered indisputable in the eyes of Muslims.

For that reason, they would often harass him. Once, when Baruch and his five-year-old son Moshe went to buy wool for weaving, Moshe saw the Muslim seller place his foot on the scales to add weight. His father,

who was short-sighted and hard of hearing, didn't notice a thing. Moshe, who witnessed his own father being conned, chose instinctively to remain silent. On the way back he told his father what he had witnessed.

'It's better that you said nothing,' his father told him.

When they arrived home, his wife Aze saw that the wool was worth less than what they had paid.

'What happened to the wool?' she asked. 'Why did you bring back so little?'

'The blessing was taken away from the wool,' Baruch replied. Aze understood him and said nothing, and this went on for years.

Another instance occurred on a Friday. Baruch walked out to his orchard. Muslims were waiting for him and beat him furiously until he passed out. When he didn't return home for the Sabbath, his family members realized something must have gone wrong, but since the Sabbath had already started and the orchard was well beyond the Sabbath border, they couldn't go out and look for him.

Moshe, who was 23-years-old and married to his first wife, Esther, sent two of his Muslim workers to the orchard. They found him unconscious with numerous bodily injuries. They placed him on a horse and brought him home. For two days he laid at home, unconscious. When he came to, he told his family what had happened.

'It happened in the afternoon,' Baruch said. 'Suddenly, a small rock was thrown at me from the back. When I turned around to see who threw it, I saw no one. I kept working. Another stone was thrown, and then another. When I turned I saw a huge man.

The man said to me, 'I am an angel. I've come to ask you what you're doing out here at this hour. You are well beyond the Sabbath border, and you will never be able to get back home in time.' He began hitting me, lifting me with his hands and throwing me on the ground. That's probably when I lost consciousness...'

Moshe realized immediately that this could not have been the true account of that day. He had no doubt that the Muslim workers ambushed his father; they had been planning to take his land from him for a long time.

Baruch asked everyone except his eldest, Moshe, to step outside. He sent for the manager of the workers. When the manager arrived, Baruch asked him what they wanted from him.

The manager replied, 'You will keep the lands and the orchards. We will keep working. But we shall do it as partners. You can sell the goods, but we will split the profit equally.'

Moshe, who was in good terms with the Barzani family, promptly paid a visit to Mustafa Barzani, who was then only 15-years-old, and told him the story. Mustafa, who was already an all-powerful ruler over the region, immediately wrote a proclamation to be delivered by his men. The text included just one line, and left no room for doubt. It read, 'Whoever dares raise a hand over my beloved Jews, I shall behead him with my very own hands.'

Naturally, the Muslims ceased harassing Baruch and his family, and continued to work for them as before.

After Baruch passed away, his three sons inherited his orchards, vineyards and fields. Moshe, the eldest, received half the property. The other half was split between his other two sons, David and Benyamin. Moshe, who already had some capital of his own, quickly bought out his two brothers, who were not interested in agriculture. David was a weaver and Benyamin worked as a stableman, escorting brides to their weddings. Both sons were thrilled to get rid of the land and receive the money, which was far more useful to them.

Moshe, on the other hand, went to work the fields with the Muslims in the same way his father had. He still felt that the Muslims wanted to dispossess him from his lands, so he saved as much money as he could, trading

silver for gold coins, knowing the wisdom of saving for a rainy day.

This habit quickly became an obsession, and he infected his whole family with his frugality, or thriftiness. He became so miserly that he began scolding his wife for using too much meat in the kubbeh. 'I could do without the meat,' he would shout. 'You should use more vegetables and save the meat!'

As the eldest of Baruch's sons, Moshe was the leader of the entire family. He had two sons from his first wife. His firstborn was named Levy, but changed his name to Abd al Rahman after converting to Islam. The other was Gedalya, nicknamed "Gado". Moshe also had two daughters: Hisne and Rande.

After the passing of his first wife, Esther, he married again. His second wife's name was Mahbube and she gave him two sons, Barkuna and Gribo. Barkuna was one year older than his cousin Shamca, and a year and a half older than his brother Gribo.

Despite his riches, Moshe was a difficult man. He lorded over the family and never helped his brothers, David and Benyamin. His grasp was so tight that he wouldn't release a single penny, or rather, a single dirham, even when he saw how hard his brothers had it - their children wearing rags and walking barefoot.

Moshe was a shrewd trader who could talk to the Kurds in their own trading language. They loved him and valued him as an honest and fair man and trader.

Abd al Rahman, Moshe's oldest, was born in 1905 or 1906. He was two years older than his brother Gedalya, or Gado. His Hebrew name was Levy, but everyone called him Ad Rahman. He was born in Barzan, during a time that was not at all easy for the Jews. This was during the death rattles of the Ottoman Empire, as the two major empires - the British and the French - were gradually biting off its lands. World War I was drawing near.

The Ottoman Empire's rule grew weaker and weaker, particularly in regions distant to the hub of the empire. This weakening was felt around Barzan too, and it manifested in general chaos, which was often expressed in the harassment of Jews and other minorities. During those years, Zere's father, Haim and his brother, Isaac were both murdered.
In 1903 Mustafa Barzani was born in Barzan. The relationship between the Barkuna and Barzani families created a strong friendship between the Mullah, Abd al Rahman and Gado. Their friendship grew over the years until one day, at age fifteen, Abd al Rahman decided to convert to Islam - mostly as a tribute to his friend Barzani, but also due to the Muslim attitude towards the Jews.
All of his family's attempts to talk him out of the conversion went unheard. Abd al Rahman stuck with Barzani, traveling with him around the villages and towns where his forces were located. Sometimes, when he wasn't walking around with Barzani, he would come back to his parents' house in Barzan and live as a Jewish man at home and as a Muslim man in public.
When Gado turned 18 he married Chizeme and moved with her to Presa, a town near Barzan. His brother also moved in with them. During the great escape from Barzan in 1931, when Hisne's family ran to Harrana, Moshe and his family - including Abd al Rahman and

Gado - fled to Akra. The money they brought with them and their friendship with Mustafa Barzani enabled them to acclimate quickly and easily.
Abd al Rahman, who lived adjacent to his father, traded in everything he could get his hands on, but mostly in wool, carpets and coats with hoodie-like hats. He also built special devices that porters carried on their shoulders, using wool to ease the bearing of the loads. These were called "cappana", meaning: shoulder.
He also traded in grains including wheat, buckwheat, and chickpeas, and owned cattle, horses and donkeys. Every season, he arranged for the crops from his father's fields in Barzan to be delivered directly to his father in Akra, fully supported by the Mullah.
One day Abd al Rahmani fell in love with a married Muslim woman. He was an impressive man: tall, sturdy, always wearing new and clean clothes. He would also adorn himself with colorful kaffiyehs and bonnets. His friendship with the Mullah added to his status and to the respect everyone had for him, as did the fact that he was Moshe's son - as Moshe soon became one of the most influential people in town.
In fact, the entire Barkuna family, who arrived at Akra with all their sons: Moshe, David and Benyamin, as well as their wives, sons, and daughters - had become a powerful force in town.
Abd al Rahman took care of all the family's needs. In time, he began to behave like a Muslim in every way, but would occasionally sneak out to see Hisne or Chizeme and eat some Jewish food that reminded him of his home and his childhood.
Most of all he loved pishke - the ground beef that is the basis of many Kurdish dishes. With the pishke, they would cook even simple dishes such as fried egg. This taste would send him right back to his childhood and fill his body and his spirit with renewed energy. Abd al Rahman loved Chizeme immensely, and always stood

beside her when Gado, his brother, beat her.

His love for the Muslim woman only increased his affinity for Islam. If there had ever been the slightest chance of his return to Judaism, surely now it was gone for good.

The couple's affair had not gone unnoticed by the Muslims in the area, and particularly by the woman's family. She later divorced her husband, but Abd al Rahman's friendship with Mustafa Barzani's family, and his own family (which was very large), prevented the Muslims from harming him.

Other factors that helped keep him safe included his business connections and that he took care of the needs of many Muslim families. Barzani, who visited Akra many times, would declare again and again that anyone who would dare raise a hand to his Jews would be beheaded. The phrase 'my Jews' was often cited by him.

Over the years, one after another passed away: Benyamin, Abd al Rahman's uncle, and his father Moshe. In 1941, following Moshe's death, David and his family left Akra and moved to Baghdad. Of the entire family, the only ones still in Akra were Benyamin's wife and daughters, Gado, Grib and Barkuna - Abd al Rahman's brother.

A year or so later Grib left as well, with his fiancee Hisne. Gado and his family left with them. Eventually, Abd al Rahman was on his own without his family, but with the enduring respect he had gained due to his friendship with Barzani.

David and Zere had to work very hard to make a living. Their children also had to assist in supporting the family, despite their young age. David was a real incompetent, an untalented and angry man. He beat his wife and children often.

When things didn't quite go his way or he would fail at something, it would result in a beating.
Shamca, being the only son, had to work very hard. He did not yet have any male siblings, and at five years old he was already gathering wood for the fire. He was forced to do difficult manual labor, labor fit for a grown man - not a five-year-old boy.
The ruler over the home from a young age was his sister Hisne. That was just how things were in Kurdistan in those days. Young children were forced to carry the family burden, never having the chance to know what a real childhood felt like.
Hisne was a beautiful and clever girl. Her beauty helped her, but could sometimes be harmful. It brought her a lot of trouble over the years. She was the undisputed leader of the entire gang of children, and served as a leader in the family as well. Even as a young child she had intuition - almost foresight, one might say. Her kind advice always helped.
Shamca couldn't do anything without Hisne's help. Sarah was more independent, though she was only three or four-years-old, but Shamca was entirely dependent on Hisne. She was the one who decided where they went, what they did, when they worked and when they played. This was how David and Zere's home was run, in the shadow of rich Uncle Moshe.
Hisne and Shamca didn't like Uncle Moshe. They never forgave him for one traumatic, brutal night that occurred many years prior. Shamca was three or three-and-a-half-years old at the time; Hisne was five. Usually that is too young to remember anything - with the exception

of a trauma like theirs. Sarah was only two, and she has no memory of it.

"It was twilight hour," Hisne told me many years later. "The sun had just sat and darkness was starting to spread. Two men arrived at our doorstep. I immediately recognized Uncle Moshe, who entered first, and his son, Gado, who followed after. Gado was about eighteen at the time, and looked a lot like his father."

Hisne portrays them both as very tall and broad, with low voices.

"Even when they spoke quietly, without raising their voice, everyone would listen," she explained. "Moshe had a thick beard all the way down to his chest. It added to his threatening appearance, as did the respect everyone had for him. Gado was just as scary - he was known as someone who was not afraid of anything."

Hisne paused and slowly sipped her tea.

"Gado walked the Muslim villages around Barzan, even those that took a few days of walking to arrive at. He slept and ate in the fields, and walked. Only rarely did he ride a donkey."

Hisne described the event like it happened yesterday.

"They both walked in. Moshe entered first, growling at my mother in a threatening tone: 'Mato gmrati la! Mani wat daamrati la,' meaning: How dare you say no to me! Who are you to say no to me? My mother, who was sitting on the ground, occupied - can't recall with what - must have realized what the men had come for. She leapt from her seat and stood up in front of them. At that moment, Moshe attacked her and began hitting her face and head. Gado joined in, kicking her legs and punching her stomach. Little Shamca cried out, 'Yimi, yimi, yimi': my mother! I ran over and hugged him as hard as I could, crying loudly; I don't remember whether I've ever cried as loud as I did that day. The skies must have ripped apart at the sound of my cries.

Two-year-old Sarah woke up, startled, and began

weeping. Shamca and I held each other and cried. But we were in for a horrifying and heartbreaking twist: my father, who was supposed to protect my mother, joined in and started beating her too. Our horror combined with confusion, and our crying grew stronger.

My mother, who was in an advanced stage of pregnancy, fell to her knees. Her face bleeding, she wept, 'Mteli eba mteli eba': I understand, I understand. At that very moment, the beating ceased. Uncle Moshe hissed at her, 'Kadome madyata chalntach lakha'; tomorrow you'll bring your sister here. The men left, but not before Gado pushed away my mother's head in contempt.

My father then hissed at my mother as well, 'Iyala, iyala. Akhtun lay fahmenun gera': That's the way... you just don't understand it any other way. My mother got to her feet and came to us. She picked us up in her arms, both of us hugging and crying. Little Sarah was also collected into my mother's embrace. We remained in that position for a long time. I don't remember how we fell asleep that night, but it must have been in that state: hugging and shaking from fear and from crying."

Hisne took another sip from her tea and went on. "The cause of the horrible scene that night was Gado's desire to marry Chizeme, my mother's sister," Hisne explained. "My mother was Chizeme's legal guardian after the death of their parents. My mother's family, generally, did not reach old age. My mother's parents, Haim and Hisne Adony, were the offspring of Asenath Barzani. They married young and had four children. My own mother, Zere, was the eldest. After her came two boys and then Chizeme, the younger sister. The two boys died of starvation when they were young, but my mother survived. Shortly after their death, their father Haim was murdered.

One day when he and Isaac went out looking to make some money for the family, they were met by thieves. Thieves were very common around the mountains, and would often murder people while robbing them of the simplest of things such as food, some silver or gold, or simply because the person was Jewish.

When they failed to return home, everyone understood what had happened. Hisne, my grandmother, Haim's wife - for whom I was named - started calling out 'Nijda kpla ebu': They were hurt by robbers. The entire family immediately went out to look for them, and two days later their bodies were found in the river, entangled in branches on the river bank.

Needless to say, no police force existed there, nor any sort of organization or central government to represent all the villages. No muhtar or sheik could do anything against the robberies and certainly not against the killing of the Jews, a phenomenon the Muslims took for granted.

Less than a year after the brothers were murdered, my grandmother Hisne died from a mysterious illness, perhaps from grief. My family almost entirely ceased to exist."

After another short break, Hisne went on to tell me about her mother's family.

"The Beit-Adony family was a very privileged family. It was almost holy. Every generation had its mekubals and rabbis. One of the family members was Asenath Barzani, who was known as Asenath the Tanna'it. She was a real rabbi, head of her yeshiva.

When did she live..? Oh, many years ago. Maybe four hundred years, maybe more. Mualem Zacharya used to say that my mother, Zere, was the descendent of a holy family.

Asenath's father, Rabbi Samuel Barzani, was a great mekubal. He was known all over Kurdistan. He established his own yeshiva. His daughter Asenath married the very best student in the yeshiva. His name was Rabbi Jacob Mizrahi. After Rabbi Samuel died, Jacob was made head of the yeshiva.

Rabbi Samuel was so important in my family, that whenever my father had to swear over something, it would always be either Jerusalem or Rabbi Samuel's grave. He called him 'babo sava.' We visited his grave several times a year. And Asenath - you wouldn't believe it - she also studied in the yeshiva. When her husband died, she replaced him; she was head of the yeshiva."

I heard the story of Asenath the Tanna'it and her relation to us many, many times. It was told with pride at any opportunity. Hisne admired her, perhaps even saw her as a role model.

"Things are different today," she told me. "Today everyone can read and write. But back then only a few could, and certainly no women could. Asenath could read, write, even rule on halachot. She was among the greatest scholars of her time and knew many secrets of the Kabbalah. After she died, everyone would visit her grave in Amadiya."

Life expectancy in the Kurdistan mountains was very short: the average was around 45-50 years. In those days no medical knowledge or medicine was available in the region.

"After my grandmother Hisne, my mother's mother, passed away, someone had to take care of the two orphans she left behind. Zere, my mother, was 12-years-old. Her sister Chizeme was only four. 12-year-old Zere married David of the Baruch-Barkuna family, taking her sister under her wing.
When Chizeme turned 12, Gado began lusting after her and asked to marry her. Moshe, his father, agreed that it was high time to marry off his son. Zere objected to the idea and tried to talk Chizeme into refusing.
'It's bad enough that I have to suffer this family, being married to David,' she told Chizeme. 'You can see for yourself how awful they are. Everything is done by brute force. Beatings are the solution for everything. I don't want you to marry him, and I don't want you to suffer as I do.'
Zere decided that the best solution would be to keep Chizeme as far away from home and her husband's family as possible. At the very first chance, she sent Chizeme away with a trader convoy to Akra. There was a Jewish orphanage of sorts that was run by the head of the community, Khwaja Khano. Khanu took it upon himself to save Jewish girls from marrying Muslims - as far as his financial state allowed.
It was this act by Zere which caused that horrible scene which little Hisne and Shamca witnessed. Eventually Chizeme was brought back to Barzan, married Gado and they lived together in Presa, a nearby village.
Gado loved Chizeme with all his heart and gave her everything she wanted. He wrapped her in gold: bought her golden earrings, golden bracelets and a large golden necklace. He bought her the finest clothes. But every

rose has its thorn; Gado was an incredibly jealous man. He wouldn't let Chizeme talk or even look at another man without his permission. Nor did he allow her to leave the house without permission, even to visit neighbors. Any breaking of the rules on her side led to a horrible fight and to verbal and physical violence. Chizeme had to live that way for years: immensely beloved but completely devoid of freedom.

Meanwhile, David and Moshe's five little children grew up. The family's relationship with Mustafa Barzani was a great help to them. Whether they needed financial aid, security, or food, they turned to him. All five children: Hisne, Shamca and Sarah (David and Zere's children) and Barkuna and Grib (Moshe's children) - were born between 1922-1925. Age differences were a year and a half, at most.

The five grew up together, played together, worked together, fought together; they did everything together. And they did it all in between bombings by the British and the Arabs, aimed at Mustafa Barzani.

It is important to note that the Kurds are not Arabs. They are a people in their own right. They have their own character, their own dress, their own food and their own language. The Arabs are an entirely different people. They speak a different language, dress differently, eat differently. While it's true that they share a religion - Islam - in every other way, they are two separate peoples.

A great war took place between the Kurds and the Arabs. In those days Iraq was yet to exist, as were Syria, Jordan and Saudi Arabia. The Ottoman Empire ruled the region and was gradually being taken over by the British and the French. The British divided the Ottoman Empire's Arabic region into countries, and crowned kings in each. Some of those kings were members of the same family. That is how Saudi Arabia, Iraq, Syria and Jordan were created. In fact, this entire divided Arabic empire was a people in its own right: a single race of Arabic people, separated from the race of Kurds. This is why the war between the Kurds and the Arabs was a war between two peoples, long before the region was split into countries."

When Hisne told stories of life in Kurdistan, she always said that she didn't know exactly what the Arabs wanted from Mustafa Barzani. I asked her, "Why do you say Arabs? They are Iraqis." Hisne replied that Iraqis or Syrians did not exist back then - they were all Arabs. "Also," she added, "Arabs are black and Kurds are white. Can't you see that?"

In those days, I was a 13-year-old bar mitzva boy and Hisne was just starting to share her stories with me; I knew nothing of the split Arab empire. Many years later, having learned the history of the region and studied the subject, I knew well what she had meant.

Shamca used to say that between one Arab strike on Mustafa Barzani's forces to the other, life in Barzan continued as normal. The three boys - he and his brothers, Barkuna and Grib - were favored by Barzani. They amused him.

Shamca, who looked a lot like Hisne, had brown hair which bounced on his neck whenever he walked or ran. He had brown-green eyes that spread terror when he was angry or upset about anything. He was a strong child and a little bully, compared to Barkuna or Grib. Barkuna was very thin, and Grib, who looked a little healthier than Barkuna, was much younger and also taller and fuller. Both were weaker than Shamca.
When he had time to spare, Mustafa sent his bodyguard or one of his assistants to bring the three boys to him. He encouraged them to wrestle in his room. He particularly enjoyed watching Shamca knock the other two down, stack them one on top of the other, and sit on them with a victorious smile.
Barzani would burst out laughing and ask for a rematch, except this time Shamca would lie on his stomach and the other two would sit on him and hold his hands. The fight began in that position, despite Shamca's protests. Barzani would cheer him on, for even in this state he could still easily overtake the other two. And indeed, the fight would be decided in his favor within seconds. Shamca soon had the other two back on the ground, sitting on top of them, while Barzani roared with laughter all the while.
Playing with the boys made Barzani very happy. He encouraged them to keep fighting - with Shamca on all fours, Grib strangling him, and Barkuna holding his feet from behind. And again, Shamca would beat them both, and Barzani would laugh.
'You're a real man, Shamca,' Barzani would say happily. 'You're not a boy, you're a man.' Shamca was five-years-

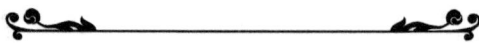

old, Grib was four-and-a-half, and Barkuna was six, at the time.

The family's ties to Mustafa Barzani were very strong. The children played with him often and he knew every one of them by name.

Hisne told me that one day her mother sent her to Barzani to ask for a few radishes. She walked over to him, after getting the approval of his bodyguard, of course.

"Mother asked for a couple of radishes," Hisne said. In Kurdish and Arabic, when someone asks for a couple of something, they mean many - more than two. For instance, Iraqis would say 'T'eeni fat inbaiten': Give me two grapes, but were actually asking for a whole bunch. Mustafa called his bodyguard over, whispered in his ear, and the bodyguard left for the garden, returning with two radishes.

'Give them to the girl,' instructed Mustafa Barzani.

Hisne smiled, embarrassed. 'This is not enough, ya Sheikh, we're a big family.'

'But you asked for two,' he replied.

'Yes,' confirmed Hisne, trying to explain herself, 'but that's just a figure of speech...'

'You said two - you got two!' joked Barzani.

'But it's not enough,' insisted Hisne.

Barzani burst out laughing and instructed the bodyguard: 'Give her as many as she can carry.'

The guard went out to the garden, Hisne in his footsteps. He tore a large amount of radishes from the ground, as many as Hisne could possibly carry with her two hands. Meanwhile, Barzani came to the door and called her over.

'Tell your mother she should tie a kerchief around your head,' he said. 'You're a big girl now and it's inappropriate to walk bareheaded.'

Hisne was seven or eight years old. Her light and smooth hair fell over her shoulders; she had healthy

and full hair. Her honey-colored eyes and her fair skin contributed to a look that no one could ignore.

Hisne returned home with the radishes and told her mother what Mustafa had said.

'Yes,' said Zere. 'I know. I've thought long ago of asking you to cover your head.'

Zere was not blind to Hisne's glaring beauty, but she postponed doing anything until someone else brought it up. That's how things were in those days. Zere pulled a colorful scarf from a garment box and handed it to Hisne, who in a few quick moves, gathered her hair into it.

The children, who worked very hard, occasionally found time to play. What kind of games existed back then?

Toys were nowhere to be found, so children played with rocks. One of the most popular games was the "rakwa", meaning: piggyback ride. Every child chose a nice round stone, about the size of a fist. All stones were placed a few meters apart. Each child had to hit another's rock with their own. The loser gave the hitter a piggyback ride from the point where the rock hit, all the way to where it stopped rolling. That's why they chose round rocks - to make sure they would roll as far away as possible.

Another game was called "bakshe", which was similar to what we now call the "five stones game".

But the best games of all were the ones that were determined by the changing of the seasons. When winter came and brought snow, shepherds would spread the news as they descended with their herds to the valleys south of Barzan. The erected their tents in the valleys because there wasn't as much snow as on the mountain tops.

When snow began falling and accumulating in the fields and the slopes, the children would go sledding. Climbing up the hills was very hard - nearly impossible because of the deep snow. In order to climb they had to improvise original methods and techniques.

"Your father Shamca was the champion of climbing the snowy hills," Hisne declared. "He would take three wooden boards, each one of them about 80 cm long. He placed them on the snow, one board at a time. He then stepped on each board, in order to harden the snow underneath it. In this way he created stairs in the snow. He went up and up, transferring each board, until he reached the top. Then he would sit on one of the boards, hold the other two in his hands, and slide down the slope. The children would also play war games in the snow, and of course they built snowmen, castles, igloos and more."

When the snow melted, water filled the streams, brooks and ponds which the waterfalls created. The children would play water games. Their favorite activity was jumping from cliffs into the pond water. Shamca excelled at this activity as well, though the other brave children did their best to impress by also jumping off the high cliffs.

"I tried just as hard," Hisne recalled. "I would climb up to the cliff tops - up to three, four, even five meters high - and jump into the pools. Once, a village woman passed by and saw me - a seven- or eight-year-old girl - jumping into the water.
'You're a girl,' she shouted at me. 'You're a girl; you shouldn't be doing that! Bad things can happen to you... you don't even know what things!'
Children wore thick trousers back then and over them, a 'deshdasha' - better known today as a 'jalabiya'.
That woman went to my mother and told her I was jumping into pools. My mother only nodded her head, half-smiling, and responded 'Don't worry - I'll talk to her.' My mother knew me well. She knew I was a responsible girl and that I wouldn't do anything foolish. She knew that every risk I took was well-calculated to make sure that I wouldn't get hurt.
Even so, she waited for me to return home and asked me to cease this activity, 'At least when others can see you... it gives us a bad name. We are Jews, you know...'
'I know,' I told her. 'I know it all. I know that they look at us differently, I know it's a problem. But Muslims like us too.' And indeed, a close relationship existed between Kurdish Muslims and Jews, so much so that they would celebrate our holidays with us. We also celebrated with them. Best of all was when they would pick fruits and vegetables on a Sabbath, they would pick some for us as well and place them on our doorstep so that we wouldn't have to desecrate the Sabbath. That's right:

the Muslims helped us keep the Sabbath all the way back in the 1920s.

In our family, holidays were mostly celebrated in my mother's family home. They didn't live with us in Barzan, but resided in a nearby village, Presa. My mother's family had more members who could read, and knew how to administer the holiday traditions and ceremonies.

For instance, every Passover the entire family would celebrate the holiday in Presa with the two brothers, Elyia and Jacob. Elyia was married to Rivka, my mother's aunt.

Presa was about half a day's walk from Barzan. We needed to arrive a full two weeks before Passover for two reasons. The first was that the journey included passing through a difficult water stream. The closer it was to spring, the more it had risen following the melting of the snow. The second reason was the need to prepare for the holiday: bake the matzot from a special flour, prepare the utensils (hagalah) and clean the house.

The Passover ritual dinner was hosted by Mualem Zacharya, who was related to my mother. I remember the holidays we spent there as if it were yesterday. Mualem Zacharya's stories were wonderful. He had a great talent of describing the characters so well that we could actually picture them in our mind's eye. We felt like we were actually there with pharaoh's daughter raising Moses...observing Eliezer fulfill his duty in searching for Isaac's spouse...witnessing Hiram I, the prophet Elijah, and Mashiach ben David...

When the holiday ended and it was time to return home, we had to determine the right place and the right time to ensure that water passage was as easy as possible. There were years when we remained in Presa for a whole month, sometimes even longer, just so we could cross the river safely.

We were sitting in Hisne's apartment in Jerusalem - a standard Jerusalem-stone house containing a one-bedroom apartment with high ceilings, surrounded on both sides by a well-tended garden. The garden contained plum trees, mint, parsley, pumpkins, and basil, which Grib planted and tended.
Kochava and Ruti, Hisne's daughters, prepared kubbeh dumplings of all types and flavors: fried, baked, cooked in a soup, and steamed. Served with them were bowls of rice, grits, cooked wheat, poultry, and beef, which Hisne had prepared.

Rays from the afternoon sun shone through the windows. Sarah, Hisne's sister, entered the room and sat with us at the table. Sarah never arrived empty handed. She was carrying two baskets which contained a few warm pita breads, tomatoes, and fresh green onions.
After we ate, the stories began flowing again.
"For all the beautiful and picturesque descriptions, the place in which we were living was a God-forsaken area, far from any progress or modernity," Hisne began. "Sanitary conditions were very low. Medicine was non-existent. It was difficult to be clean and hygienic, even if you wanted."
"Remember when I got eczema on my feet?" asked Sarah.
"Of course I do," Hisne replied, and began a new story. "When Sarah was four-years-old, she got severe eczema on both her feet."
"Let me tell it," Sarah interrupted, and wouldn't let Hisne continue.
"I got eczema on both my feet. None of the medications they tried on me in Barzan helped," she told us. "They used plants and oils, but mostly prayers and spells - even talismans...that was the kind of medicine we had then."
I turned on my recording device.

After making sure that the recorder as working, Sarah continued. "Seeing that nothing was helping, my father decided to take me to Sheikh Shirita. My father was told that only Sheikh Shirita could handle these things."
"Shirita - was that the Sheikh's name?" I asked.
"I don't know," replied Sarah. "Perhaps it was the name of the village in which he lived - maybe his own name. Anyway, the distance to his village was a five- or six-hour walk. My father decided we should travel overnight, because of the heavy summer heat. Walking at night was dangerous because of the visual limitations and the threat of robbers - but it was better than walking that distance in the heat.
That evening, once it got dark, my father took a water bag and some bread, sat me on his shoulders with my aching feet hanging on his chest, and we left the village. The road wasn't paved. We walked in the dark, with only moonlight to light our way; there was a full moon. My father and I were alone in the night. Occasionally my father would stop, put me down and sit for a while. After a couple hours, he took out the bread and we ate. I wasn't hungry, but I was bothered by the pain and itching of my feet. After half an hour's rest, my father placed me on his shoulders again and we continued walking. While walking, he suddenly leapt forward.
'I heard rustling from the bushes,' I exclaimed.
'It's just a little stream,' my father replied. Only when we had arrived at the village did he tell me that it had actually been a snake.
We arrived at the village just before dawn. Everything was still dark. The villagers were sleeping and we had to wait a while until the village began its daily routine. My father asked around for the sheikh's address. When we arrived at his home, he greeted us kindly and didn't even ask my father what was the matter. He immediately noticed my aching feet.
'Follow me,' he said.

We followed him to the attic of his house. 'Here you will be sleeping for the next three days,' he told my father. Meanwhile, he called in a servant and asked that he fetch sweet pomegranate peels. The servant immediately departed. When he returned, the sheikh took the peels out to the yard and crushed them with a "sitta", a stone alcove found in every family's yard, that was used for grinding wheat and removing the chaff.

"Once he finished grinding the peels until they were almost as soft as pulp, he asked the servant to bring "masta", a type of goat-milk cheese that looks like thick yoghurt. He mixed the masta with the pomegranate peels and applied the mixture to both of my feet and ankles, halfway up my shins.

'You've been walking all night, now go get some sleep,' the sheikh said to my father. He instructed him to lay me down so that my feet didn't touch each other and leave me that way until he returned.

We were so tired from the long journey that we fell asleep immediately. Someone placed something under my head, but my father fell asleep on the floor with only his hands as a pillow. When evening came and we awoke, the servant entered, carrying bread, figs, raisins and water. This would be our menu for all three days we spent in the sheik's home. Every morning he would come in and wash my feet and re-apply his ointment. While he washed them, I noticed my feet grow redder and redder, as if they were dripping blood. The burning sensation was almost too painful to bear.

I restrained myself with all my strength. I didn't cry or speak a word, only twisted my face with pain. Three days later, the redness and the itching began to taper off. 'There,' said the sheikh. 'It's getting better.' He again called his servant. 'I've decided to send these people home,' he told him. He instructed my father to keep rubbing my feet with the ointment. He also offered him

some pomegranate peels, but my father assured him we had plenty of them at home.

'In that case, just keep rubbing her feet the same way,' he said. 'In a few weeks, with the help of Allah, all will work out.' He turned to his servant once more, ordering him to carry me on his shoulders halfway to Barzan. There he would hand me to my father and return to the village.

So, that's exactly what he did. He carried me halfway as his master had instructed. The return home was much easier. When we arrived, my father continued treating me with the ointment. A few weeks later the eczema had disappeared."

We finished our meal.

"What would you like to drink, Kapara?" asked Hisne and didn't wait to hear the answer. Kochava handed us glasses of dark tea and sugar cubes on a small plate. She served date cookies to us, and salty crackers to Hisne, who had recently developed diabetes.

"Remember the Barzan snakes?" asked Sarah while sipping her tea.

"Remember? Of course I do," replied Hisne. "How the town suffered from those snakes!" They came into the houses. The walls, which were made of mud bricks, couldn't stop them; nor could the roofs - made of wooden beams adhered with a mix of mud and straw - prevent them from entering.

The snakes that were poisonous, we tried to scare away or kill. My mother was the bravest. First, she would grab a hollow cane - one of those which grew on the river bank. She would cut the edge in two so that the result looked like the letter Y, take the open end and press it to the snake's throat - right under his head - pull it down from the ceiling and smash its head on a rock.

We could distinguish between different types of snakes. Those which were not poisonous were kept at home, since we believed they brought good luck. They slithered around the house uninterrupted.

Many stories and legends developed around that plague of snakes. One story that was popular in Barzan told of a bride on her wedding night who sat next to a wall while drinking her tea, and suddenly felt a stinging sensation on her head. The story is reminiscent of the Talmud story about Rabbi Akiva's daughter, and is possibly its source.

At any rate, the bride paid little attention to it. After a while, she felt another sting on her head. She asked her new husband to take a look, as she thought perhaps a hairpin was bothering her. The husband looked and found a snake peeking out from the wall and biting his new wife. Luckily, the snake was not poisonous. The husband, as so not to frighten his wife, pretended to pull a pin from her hair, then guided her away from the wall. Another story, which was probably true, was told to us by one of our neighbors. This neighbor was visiting another neighbor, who poured her a glass of tea. When she began drinking she noticed that the taste was strange and the water was oily. Of course she didn't drink the remainder. When she mentioned it to her host, the two of them took a look at the water in the samovar. When they lifted the lid, they were amazed to find a snake, curled up around itself, being cooked by the boiling water. Naturally, they threw away the samovar, which was now impure."

The armed mutiny, which began in 1927, initially operated as a guerrilla war, with stakeouts and remote sniping directed at Iraqi forces. Three years later, in 1930, a turnaround occurred following the British-Iraqi agreement that gave Iraq its independence. The agreement, however, made no promises to minorities, least of all to the Kurds. The armed fighting intensified. As a result, so did the bombings of Barzan. The Kurdish fighters' guerrilla actions increased immeasurably.

During the ongoing struggle Moshe and David turned to Mustafa Barzani and asked to fight by his side.
'Absolutely not!' replied Barzani. 'My dear Jews, my beloved Jews… I believe in you much more than I ever could believe in the Arabs. Surely you remember how my late grandfather, Abd el-Salam, asked you to pray for rain. I know you are the chosen people. When you prayed, the rain came. God loves you…but this is not your struggle. This is OUR struggle, and we will overcome. We will not give up.'
Suddenly he got up and began singing his national anthem.
That same anthem, written in Kurmanji, was sung to me by Aunt Hisne many years later, in Jerusalem. I will never forget how Hisne got up from her bed and sang her anthem so devotedly.
"Our country of mountains, trees in the top and trees in the bottom," sang Hisne with a shaking voice while translating for me.
"You shall not overcome us…we will raise our hands and leave no trace of you…we will believe no country… our memories are tough…we swear in our holy family that we will never put our weapons down as long as we remember Abd el-Salam, who was executed and still did not give up…one day we shall avenge on the Arabs…"
When Barzani finished singing, he turned to Moshe and David, 'You know that the Iraqi Arabs bomb this

place more than they do anywhere else. That is because I live here. Do yourselves and your families a favor, take them and move somewhere else while you still can. Go to Akra. It's a bigger city with more means of survival. There are a lot of Jews there, you will fit right in. Unfortunately, Barzan is slowly being destroyed. When we win and things calm down you can always come back.'

Moshe and David listened to him attentively and then each returned to his own home.

This might be a good time to say a few words about Mullah Mustafa Barzani. He was born on March 14th, 1903 to a religious priest from the Barzani family, which was named after the village Barzan. He studied Islam and its rules until he received the title of mullah, which in Iran is a title given to all religious priests.

Mustafa Barzani was a man of faith who followed the rules of the Koran closely. Like his father before him, he was a dervish follower. The dervishes were seen as saints by both the Sunni and the Shia Kurds; they believed them to have a direct dialog with God.
Mustafa followed a long line of warriors and leaders which came from the Barzani family. The first of them (in recent memory) was Sheikh Sayed Barzani, or Abd el-Salam, as he was known by the Kurds. The Turks made him Governor of Sulaymaniyah, but he agitated the locals against them, and in 1909 he was captured and executed.
His sons, Mahmud and Qadir followed in his footsteps. Mahmud, who was similarly made Governor of Sulaymaniyah by the British - who conquered Iraq during World War I, stuck to the idea of an independent Kurdistan. He directed propaganda against the British, and for that reason was sent to exile (and eventually, death) in Nasiriyah, which is located in swampy southern Iraq, in the Shaat al Arab area.
Several months after his death and after the revolt was suppressed, the Kurds rebelled again, this time led by brothers Ahmed and Mustafa Barzani. Mustafa, the more qualified of the two, took the lead. With his unique charisma he swept the entire Kurdish region into a long and exhausting fight against Iraq.
During the fights there were intervals of peace as well. During one of them, which was longer than the others, Moshe suggested to his brother David that they buy a cow. 'Since we've decided to stay in Barzan, we should

probably purchase a cow,' he suggested.

In Kurdistan it was customary that once a year, or once every few months, a few families would get together to purchase an entire cow. The slaughterer would walk around between the villages, slaughter the cow, and divide it into parts by the amount of money each family had paid. The internal organs were shared between all buyers, and those would be eaten within days of the purchase. The liver, heart, lungs and other internal parts were hard to preserve with the lack of cooling devices. The carcass, on the other hand, was diced - including the fat - and cooked in huge pots with a lot of salt. If the cow was not fat enough they would add sesame oil to the pot. Cooking continued for hours upon hours, until the meat was dark brown and floating in the fat. At this point, they would chop a lot of onion and add it to the stew until it became a golden color. This stew was called kaliya. The meat cuts inside the kaliya were called pishke and the fat was called zoma.

Essentially, kaliya was preserved meat stored in large jugs. The congealed fat could preserve the meat for an entire year without losing freshness. Kaliya acted as a key ingredient in most dishes, such as tarpe silke - a beet-leaf dish. Naturally, they didn't use it for stews containing milk.

There was never a shortage of vegetables. One of the most popular was beet leaves. They would brew them in boiling water. When they removed all the water, they added some kaliya - including the pishke, and cook it all together with chopped onion. Before the cooking was complete, they added beaten eggs and continue cooking for a few minutes more. This dish was considered one of the top delicacies of rural Kurdistan from that era. It was eaten with akhma rakika, a thin pita bread baked on the saj. Even simple omelettes were fried in kaliya. Some added herbs and two or three cubes of the pishke. Curry was one of the wild herbs that grew in the

Kurdistan mountains, between Purim and Passover. Each region knew it by a different name: some called it cardy; Zakho Jews called it nuwa; Iraqis called it nubbeh. I believe in Hebrew it is known as luf. It is a very spicy herb that causes itching when touched, and even more so when eaten. The curry would simmer for hours in water with smoka.

Smoka, or sumac, is a red fruit which grows in bunches. The fruit is no bigger than red lentils. It is very sour, and considered one of the primary spices in Kurdish cuisine. The sourness neutralizes the curry's spiciness as well as the itching caused by eating it. This soup is a real delicacy. It is a beloved dish in Kurdistan, particularly when adding a few kutele - kubbeh balls.

No lemons were available in Kurdistan, nor was lemon salt. The sour flavor was achieved with sumac or unripe grapes. The sumac was boiled in water, then strained and added to the pot. The grapes were brewed in warm water and squeezed in cotton, and the liquids that would drip from the cotton were then added to the pot.

Kurdistan's national dish, hamusta, got its flavor from sumac or grapes. When the dish made an appearance in Israeli cuisine, this was replaced by lemon juice or lemon salt.

David and Moshe decided to stay in Barzan. And following that decision, they bought a cow and shared it between them.

Hisne recalled that the part her mother, Zere, received was immediately cut into dice, before it could spoil. The kaliya was soon underway.

"Sarah and I helped our mother with the cooking. After we were done, she moved the kaliya into big jugs, which she brought home and buried in the ground."

Thieves would often come into houses and steal food prepared by the families. They mostly stole dried food such as rice, wheat, sesame and so on. They came in at night and took the foods; that's how they fed their

families. In many cases, the food was placed in the ground for that reason.

"During the war and the bombings, my mother covered the kaliya with sealed fabric. She tied a string around the opening of the jug, dig holes in the ground, and buried the jugs in the holes."

A few weeks passed. Moshe tried to sell the land, vineyards and orchards that he owned. He tried to sell them to the highest bidder. Having failed to make a sale, and with the winds of war blowing, Barzani advised him to let them go, for now.

'We will work them, and I promise to send the crops to you in Akra, whenever possible,' Barzani offered. 'God willing, once everything settles down, you will return here and find everything waiting for you.'
The friendship that had developed between Barzani and Moshe and his sons was so strong that Moshe decided to relocate his family to Akra, trusting his property to Mustafa Barzani. He took all his gold and silver as well as a few donkeys and goats, and planned to start life over in the house he had purchased in Akra.
David, on the other hand, waited for Moshe to give him some money so he could also escape. When that didn't happen, and Moshe had already left town with his entire family, David realized there was nothing to wait for. He understood well that his life, and the lives of his family, were in danger.
After a few weeks, when the bombings intensified, he finally decided to leave. He took his wife and his five children - two more children were born after Hisne, Shmuel and Sarah: Mame, now three-years-old, and Aharon, one-and-a-half-years old, and left town.
'We're going to Akra,' he informed his wife. 'We shall arrive within a few days. There are many Jews there, alongside Muslims, Christians and the rest.' Penniless, with only the clothes on their backs, David and Zere - who was in an advanced stage of pregnancy - left for Akra with their five children.
This was during the summer of 1931. Hisne was nine years old, Shamca was seven, and Sarah was six; they were joined by the younger Mame and Aharon. They were accompanied by Elo, who tied his fortune to theirs

and chose to escape Barzan with them.

Elo was the husband of Rande, Moshe's daughter and the sister of Gado and Abd al Rahman. She was Moshe's daughter from his first wife, Esther. She and Elo had two children, a boy and a girl. Two years after the birth of her daughter, Rande developed a skin condition which included a rash that later turned into facial sores. From her face, the disease spread all over her body.

The so-called "wise" men of the region, witchdoctors and talisman writers, couldn't heal her. Rande was feverish and eventually died. Elo was left with two children, three- and four- years of age. In those days a child who lost their mother was usually given to a Muslim family, adopted and raised as a Muslim - unless the father remarried, which usually happened. In that case, the children would be raised by the stepmother or thrown out to live with relatives.

When the war broke out and the Jews relocated, Elo had only two options: either to give away his children to a Muslim family, or to take them and escape together. He chose the latter and joined David and Zere.

Once the decision was made, a new problem arose: how to carry the four babies. Sometimes the parents carried them, sometimes Hisne, sometimes Shamca. Occasionally, the young ones had to make their way by foot. The escape passed through valleys and into a place where the Iraqi bombs could never reach them.

"To be honest," Hisne confided, "I didn't know where we were going. I don't think my mother and father knew either. We walked through a narrow and deep valley which was surrounded by tall cliffs on both sides. Occasionally we saw Kurdish soldiers who were walking in the same valley. When the planes dropped bombs, we hid in the caves alongside the road. They were tiny caves, located in the bottom of the cliffs around the valley. They were sort of conclave cliffs, created by the water that ran in the valleys during flood season. The water also created pits along the river's flow path - just like the remalyia pits in the Negev desert, which were created at the bottom of flint stones.

We passed from cave to cave, all the while sharing the task of carrying the children on our backs. The whole family was walking towards the unknown.

'Mom, what will happen to all the kaliya you made?' asked Sarah during one of our stops. 'Will the Arabs eat it?'

'Don't worry,' my mother replied. 'We will return home and find it untouched.'

I looked at my mother and at Elo. I saw him frown, close his eyes and give a small, bitter smile, as if he was saying to himself: We will never return to Barzan. The bombings went on and on," continued Hisne. "One time, an airplane bombed an entire group of soldiers. I saw them fall like strawberries. Once, I even stepped out of the cave and ran to one of the dead soldiers. I thought I might find some food or money in his pockets - anything that could help us survive.

The soldier was lying on his stomach. I heard Sarah yell from behind me, 'Leka dazat khalnti?', Where are you going sister? I didn't reply. I kept running and when I got to the soldier, I turned him over. I opened his vest; his rakhta, his insides, came pouring out. I had blood all over me. I began screaming and shouting. While trying to turn the soldier over, Sarah arrived, having chased after me from the cave. The blood sprayed on her, too. She began screaming, 'Yalakh lakha', Let's go back! We looked through his clothes and vest, but found nothing but bullets. We returned to the cave. Our parents stared at us, as if asking, 'Well?'

'Nothing,' we replied, in unison.

Mother and father were determined to run away. We saw no signs of weakness or fear in their faces. So we migrated from cave to cave until the bombings ceased. In fact, we had no way of knowing whether they had stopped or rather we simply managed to get far away enough from Barzan so that we were no longer able to hear them.

Young Aharon and Mame, as well as Elo's children, (Elo followed behind us so that we wouldn't be too close), were silent the entire journey. When the bombing ceased and it was quiet, the children began crying. The hunger had gotten to them. Without food or any edible plants around, we were struck by an urgent need to get to some sort of town or village.

Shmuel, Sarah and I began searching for edible plants such as 'khubeza' - mallow, and 'balko' - notobasis," recalled Hisne. "The mallow's stalk and fruit could be eaten raw. The fruit looked like a loaf of bread, hence the name khubeza, from "khubez", meaning: bread. In Israel this plant was called 'bird's bread' for its shape. The notobasis, on the other hand, had to be peeled from its thorns. The children were very skilled at doing so, since this was their entire meal."

The Kurdistan villages were spread across the mountains, a few hours' walk between. Some villages had only a few houses, others had dozens. What usually happened was that one or two extended families resided in each village.

"On our way to find a populated area," said Hisne, "we arrived at a raging river which we had to cross. On the river bank we found a number of people on mules. They took an interest in us. When my father told them we were from Barzan, they asked whether it was still being bombed. My father replied, 'Yes'. He told them we were looking for a place to dine, since we hadn't had anything to eat since morning. Cooked food and gruel for the babies could only be found in populated places. They directed us to a nearby village, but to get there we had to cross the river, which could not be traversed with the children. The strangers volunteered their help: they placed us, the children, in bags that were hanging

from their mules. Shmuel and I insisted on crossing on our own. My father's fear-inducing stare told us that this wasn't the time to argue, and that we must do as we are told.

We were placed inside the bags on one of the mules. My mother, who was pregnant, was supported by my father and Elo. This was how we crossed the river together. We, the children, screamed in fear. We heard the rushing water below us, and we had never before ridden inside bags.

When we arrived on the other side of the river, our transporters - who were Muslim Kurds - pulled out a slice of bread, a few dried figs and some raisins. These were ingredients that every Kurd had with him when making his way around the mountains.

We sat and dined on the river bank. One of the strangers found some juicy dates for the children, to make us stronger. After we parted, we continued walking towards Bas, as we were instructed. We arrived there after an hour's walk. This was just before sunset. A woman who was busy hanging laundry to dry noticed us from afar. She stopped her work immediately and came running.

'Where have you come from, strangers?' she asked.

'Barzan,' we replied.

'Jews?'

'Yes,' my father replied.

In those times, there was friendship and camaraderie between Muslims and Jews. 'You must need a place to sleep,' said the woman.

'We do,' my mother replied.

'No problem. There is plenty of space here. We have a huge room made of wood. It used to be occupied by goats and donkeys, but it's available now.' The woman took an interest in our occupations.

'I am a weaver,' replied my father. 'I work with wool and walk around in villages, selling my products. I probably won't have any weaving work to do here, but I'm happy

to do whatever you tell me to.'

'I do laundry and agriculture,' my mother added. 'I sort wheat and rice - that's what I've done my entire life. I also help my husband spin the wool, but I will also do anything you ask of me.' And so we settled in Bas, in the large room offered to us by the local woman.

After a month of working and just barely being able to provide for ourselves, my mother gave birth. In these types of villages there were no hospitals or midwives. When a woman gave birth she was assisted by the village women. And indeed, once the children and my father left the room, women from all over the village entered and helped her. That was how we got a new sister, Nergez, or Narkis in Hebrew.

My father made a living but we were still poor. The hunger almost overpowered us. All around the village people had trouble finding work, and they all felt the poverty and the deprivation. After a few months in Bas my father decided it was time to move on to Akra. We piled up everything we owned, which was very little - mostly clothes.

By now there were eight of us: my parents, myself, Shmuel, Sarah, Aharon, Mema and Nergez. It was much harder to travel. We were told of a bigger town nearby called Harran, which was populated mostly by Christians. This was, in fact, the biblical Harran - from where Abraham left for the land of Israel. 'We will go to Harran,' my father told us. 'From there we will continue to Akra.'

And so once again we made a journey, the entire family, all the way to Harran. It was a slightly larger settlement than Bas, and in the center was a large and beautiful church. The truth is, I was so young and had seen so few buildings in my life, that the church - which was actually quite small - seemed big and impressive in my eyes. It was the most beautiful building I had ever seen. When we arrived, the locals in Harran greeted us with open arms. They were Yazidis, members of an ancient Mesopotamian religion who practiced Christian rituals as well. There, too, we were given a large wooden room with a high ceiling. 'We will stay here for a few weeks and then make our way to Akra,' my father decided. But that short stay in Harran ended up lasting three years."

Now that my parents were taking care of six children, life was even more difficult. They had eight mouths to feed, including a newborn baby whose dietary needs were obviously different.

Livelihood was nowhere to be found. My father, who knew only one type of work - how to weave with a loom - asked for some wool from the locals and began creating his famous trousers again. He sold his products in nearby villages, but the meager sums he received in exchange were not enough for us to live adequately. That was why my mother and the older children, Shmuel, Sarah and I - had to go out to the fields with the locals and gather leftovers of the vegetable and wheat crops into the baskets we brought with us. This small addition helped us survive, but only barely.
We asked the locals whether we could work for them for a paycheck, but they replied they don't work for money and so had no need for us. We acquired food by begging for it - mostly legumes - and by gleaning the fields.
"You have no idea, you don't know what we went through," recalled Hisne and patted her knee. "No angels were around us. Perhaps only the grim reaper. Only he came along to watch us and see whether he could take anyone with him."
Despite the hard times we went through, we loved the nights the most. We would gather around the fire, warm ourselves, and listen to stories. We heard the far-away howling of jackals, gurga. We sat around the fire and ate the meager amount of food we had managed to gather. Elo, who remained a widower and took care of his children with endless devotion, joined our evenings. He sat around the fire with us and told stories that fascinated us all. We could sit entire nights around the fire with him. His stories captivated not only the children - but also my parents, who would sit and listen to him attentively. One story surprised us in particular.

One night, while sitting around the fire, Elo told us that he had once traveled to the land of Israel, couldn't manage to make a living there, and returned to Kurdistan. We were shocked. Israel was always our heart's desire and we saw it as a land flowing with milk and honey. Elo continued to amaze us.

'Israel is a desert land,' he said. 'It has no water, no plants, no work, not anything. Nothing. Where are all the dates we have here? All the sweet figs? Where are the large grapes we enjoy? Here, everything grows freely in every corner. There, no one even speaks our language.'

We found it hard to believe what we had just heard.

'I guess it's not time for salvation just yet,' said Elo sorrowfully. 'I guess the almighty God has not yet prepared the land for us. Exile must go on for a while longer...we can't rush life and do things too soon.' We found great comfort in Elo's presence. We felt safer having another man around. Elo in particular was a very polite and pleasant man.

The fire wasn't only for warming us and cooking our food. It was also our place of gathering every night, and we slept around it. We slept on the ground, of course. We never had any beds. We spread fabric upon the ground and slept around the fire, like the petals of a rose: our feet by the fire and our heads farther away.

Those who could afford one, rested upon a mat called barmal, in Kurdish. This was a colorful cloth made of coarse wool, which was hung on the walls as decoration in the homes of the rich. We had no barmals: both because they were expensive and because they were heavy and difficult to carry around during travel. We made do with fabric leftovers which we spread upon the ground and slept on, after removing rocks and smoothing the soil, which had grown rough during the day.

All night long we heard the jackals' howls. My mother said they were the voices of deceased Arabs. Not far

from where we lived was a Muslim cemetery. My mother told us that Muslims didn't bury their dead deep enough, and that's why at night they stepped out of their graves and howled; this scared us out of walking around at night.

"One of the things I remember most from Harran was the red soil around the church," recalled Sarah. "The soil was so red - the reddest I had ever seen. Out of the soil we would pull a sort of tuber that looked like a potato. I saw some of those in Israel too, in the Mahane Yehuda market in Jerusalem. I don't know what they are called, but my mother would peel and cook them, and it was a real delicacy. The Christians called them 'Fruits of Miriam Adra', meaning: fruits of the Virgin Mary. It must have been some variety of the Jerusalem artichoke."

Life in Haran did not run smoothly. With a severe lack of food and a total lack of medicine, the little children began getting sick. The first was Mame, who began experiencing weakness, diarrhea, vomiting and high fever, one year after our arrival. The treatment my parents gave her did not include medication because none was available. Their treatment was ineffective, and we watched Mame slowly perish.
Including Elo, we were the only Jews in Harran. He and his two children were by our side the entire time. The locals also provided them a small room near us.
We could not sustain proper Jewish life there. While my parents did keep kosher, as far as was possible, more complex religious services such as ritual slaughter, brit milah, public prayer and other observances were not options for us. Due to the lack of Jewish burial services, my mother had no choice but to wash little Mame's body herself and bury her in the local cemetery.
"Muslim cemeteries were not like the ones we know," explained Hisne. "There were no gravestones and burial was done very simply, by my mother and father. During this whole time, taking care of Mame, my parents hadn't noticed that Aharon was also getting sicker. A few short months later he died as well, probably from pneumonia. The sad ritual of washing the body repeated itself. My

parents buried Aharon in the same cemetery, right next to Mame's grave."

'Did you bury them deep enough?' inquired Sarah, with childish naiveté.

Mother answered with a bitter cry while hitting her own face with her hands, 'I buried them very deep.'

My mother gradually began losing her sanity. Every day she hit herself in the face and cried endlessly. Her entire mind was filled with worry for Shmuel, who remained her only son, ekana in Kurdish. 'Pshlokh ekana, pshlokh ekana," she would cry, You've remained alone.

A human being has that primal instinct, just like other animals, of giving life to as many offspring as possible. In the Kurdish tradition, as in many other cultures, the son is the one to continue the family heritage. The son is the one to carry with him the family or tribal name. Now that she had buried two sons in Barzan and one in Harran, Shmuel was her only remaining son. She had to take good care of him to make sure he would continue the family line.

Once, when my mother and Sarah were on the roof, my mother in her madness tried to push her off. I noticed what was going on and began shouting 'Babi babi yalokh lakha, yimi gmandyala sara min gare': Father, father, come here quick - mother is trying to throw Sarah off the roof!' Sarah, who was holding on as best she could to the trees which covered the roof, managed to stay put. My father got to them, grabbed my mother, brought her down and managed to calm her.

A few days later, my cousin Gado came to visit. He was the kind of man who knew all the mountain roads from village to village. He wasn't afraid of anything. He was tall, broad shouldered, had a thick beard and a deep voice. He was a very impressive man.

He used to climb to the top of the mountains to find one particular and very special plant, which had fruit called epsa, which must have been some type of plant gall.

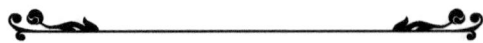

From this fruit, medicine was made. When it was ground and mixed with water, it could be made into ink. The fruit was used mostly in the leather processing industry. They would grind it, mix it with water, and soak it inside cow skins. The mixture could remove hair from the skin and also thicken it. This plant was so rare, there was a huge demand for it among witchdoctors and those who practiced folk medicine. Gado would sell the fruit for a high price - since so few could find it and identify it. Every few weeks, he would arrive at Harran. Each time he came he tried to convince my father to move to Akra. 'What are you still doing here?' he asked my parents during one of his later visits. 'We've already moved to Akra - even Moshe and Benyamin. We have a big house there: it's a bigger and more developed town, come join us.'

'We're doing very well here,' my father replied. He tried to evade the offer, since being so close to his rich brother Moshe made him uncomfortable. Sometimes it made him feel inadequate in comparison. 'But I do wish Zere would go there for a week or two, just to visit family and to see Mualem Chucha, perhaps he can give her a prayer or heal her.'

'Do you have a donkey?' asked Gado.

'No,' my father replied. 'We will have to walk.'

So my mother and father took the new baby, Nergez, and set out for Akra with Gado. The older children stayed home with Elo and his children. When they arrived at Akra, they immediately took Zere to see Rabbi Mualem Chucha. He listened to her life story, observed her and her behavior, and offered her a few prayers. He wrote a talisman on a piece of metal and hung it around her neck. He instructed her to stay with her family in Akra for at least one week.

After two weeks, my parents returned to Harran and we remained there for approximately a year. Upon their return from Akra my mother became pregnant, and we

got a new sister. My mother decided to name her Mame, after her older sister who had died the year before.

During that year, Muslims from nearby villages came to our house and asked my parents for my hand in marriage. I was eleven or twelve years old. My parents did not agree, of course - not for all the money in the world - to give me away to Muslims or Christians. Throughout the year, all sorts of attempts and tricks were made to kidnap me. One of those attempts I remember as the "wool story".

A group of young men from the village Bazi would occasionally pass through Haran. The men would stare at Hisne, sitting on the roof, spinning yarns for her father's weaving. Sometimes they would shout to her. One time, Hisne and Shmuel managed to hear how they were planning to entice her to step away from the house, and from the watchful eye of the other Harranians - particularly Shmuel - who was always by her side.

Hisne and Shmuel were like two peas in a pod. Sarah, who was nine-and-a-half years old, would usually join them, whenever she wasn't away with her father selling their goods. Shmuel never made a move without Hisne, nor did she without him. This was quite beneficial for her. Shmuel, who was eleven, was well-built, taller than Hisne, and could easily triumph over the older boys; he was Hisne's bodyguard.

Shmuel used to carry around a long pole. Sometimes he stuck a needle in the end of it. This was useful against wild animals. When he went to collect wood or work the fields, or even while walking between the villages, wolves and jackals often attacked him. He would stick the pole in the animal's mouth and it would retreat, howling in pain.

One day, the Bazi group decided to steal the wool and yarn from the rooftop. They waited for the right time. When Hisne, Sarah and Shmuel went to work in the field, they stole the lot. They weren't planning to make any use of the wool or the fabric - they wanted Hisne to leave her house and walk to Bazi in search of the stolen wool.

When the children returned from their work, they discovered that wool, fabric, and yarn were missing. 'I know just who took them,' cried Shmuel, waving his pole. 'I'm going to get them back!'

'Wait,' said Hisne. 'You're not going anywhere. That's

just what they want - for us to go searching. Along the way they will attack us and do as they want with us.'
'What do you mean?' asked Shmuel.
'What do I mean?' repeated Hisne. 'I mean they will kidnap me and kill you.' She sighed and continued. 'Do you think they mind killing a Jewish boy?'
'So what should we do?' Shmuel asked.
'We'll go to their Mukhtar, but not via the main road. We'll go see him and tell him everything. He is a kind and honest man.'
'That's true,' confirmed Sarah. 'I know him from my visits to the village with father.'
While they discussed the matter, their father stepped out and asked where all of his materials were.
'They're at Bazi,' answered Hisne. 'Shmuel and I are going to go fetch them. We'll speak to the Mukhtar.'
'Just be careful,' he ordered, and instructed Sarah to stay home.
The fields were full of pear trees. Hisne suggested they fill a bag full of fresh pears and bring it to the Mukhtar. Shmuel jumped right into the task. He grabbed an empty bag and filled it all the way with fruit. With the bag over his shoulder they began their journey.
Bazi was only an hour's walk from their house. They knew the roads well, for they had made the journey many times. This time, they took a different road - in order to prevent running into the thieves. When they arrived at the Mukhtar's house, his wife greeted them.
'How can I help you, children?' she asked.
'We've come to talk to the Mukhtar,' answered Hisne.
'He's not home right now,' responded his wife. 'Would you like to wait for him to return?'
'Yes,' Hisne replied.
'In that case," said the Mukhtar's wife, 'sit down and I'll bring you something to eat.' She served the children bread, cream and honey. They dined and waited for the Mukhtar to return home.

'Is something wrong?' his wife asked them. 'What did you come here to discuss?'

Hisne told her about the wool theft and the group of boys, but asked that she say nothing to her husband until he finished eating.

A short while later he returned home. 'Oh, what lovely guests I have!' he exclaimed with a smile. 'To what do I owe the pleasure...? How can I help you?'

'Sir,' began Hisne, 'you should eat first. Then we'll talk.'

'You are a smart girl,' replied the Mukhtar. 'I know you and your parents. You're all good Jews.'

The Mukhtar sat to eat his meal. When he finished, he sat on the floor, crossed his legs, and asked the children to tell him what had happened. Hisne told him about the group of boys who would tease her and about their theft.

'What do you have in that bag?' he asked.

'Pears,' replied Hisne. 'We brought them for you, sir.'

The Mukhtar called in his servant and ordered him to take the bag, empty it and fill it up with sesame. The servant hurried out of the room to do as he was told. He returned with a bag full of sesame seeds and placed it in front of the Mukhtar.

'Will you be able to carry this all the way home?' the Mukhtar asked Shmuel.

'Yes,' replied Shmuel, nodding his head.

'And you're not afraid to walk all the way back on your own?'

'We fear none but God,' replied Hisne.

'Come with me,' ordered the Mukhtar and stood up. He began walking, the children following. Hisne didn't even tell him who the thieving boys were - he knew by himself where he should go.

When they arrived at one of the town courtyards, he called all the residents to step outside. About 20 people came out, among them the gang of young boys. The Mukhtar looked around and asked, 'Who stole wool, fabric and yarn from these children?'

The courtyard was silent. No one said a word.
The Mukhtar looked back at Hisne and asked, 'How much would you say your stolen goods are worth?'
'15 dinars,' she answered, without hesitation.
The Mukhtar raised his eyes to the gang leader's father and said, "Get out 15 dinars right now and give it to these children.' The man looked at his son and without pause retrieved 15 dinars from his pocket, placed them in Shmuel's hand, and looked back at his son again.
The boy ran inside the house. He retrieved the stolen goods, which were tied up in a blanket, and threw them toward Hisne and Shmuel. Hisne looked at the pile and said, 'If these are our goods, I don't want the 15 dinars; my father will not accept it.'
'Tell your father that the 15 dinars are not payment for the goods,' replied the Mukhtar. 'They are a fine paid for the theft and for the trouble it has caused you.'
'Thank you so much, sir,' Hisne responded. 'You're a brave and honest man.'
'I thank you too, smart girl. You may leave.'
Hisne loaded the pile of fabrics and wool onto her back. Shmuel took the bag of sesame on his, hid the money in his pocket and together they left town.
The walk home was much easier, despite the heavy load, since the two were in high spirits. After an hour they reached Haran.
'I see you've brought it all back,' noted their father, who had been waiting for them outside the entire time.
'We have,' said Shmuel as he put down the bag of sesame seeds. 'We also brought you the 15 dinars that was paid as a fine,' he added, searching his pocket for the money. His father took the money and stepped inside, while Zere took the bag of sesame. The children looked at each other, smiled and went up on the roof to return the wool. The next day the boys appeared again, riding three donkeys. They stopped in front of the house. Hisne and Shmuel were on the roof, combing the wool with an iron

comb. Shmuel, who noticed them first, leapt to his feet and grabbed a stick.

'Throw away that stupid stick, kid!' called the gang leader. 'With or without it, I will kick your ass.'

'What do you want from us?' called out Hisne. 'We're Jewish, I'm not allowed to marry a Muslim.'

'Who even wants you? You're just a "kahba", a whore. We're here for revenge, because you went to the Mukhtar. Why should we get punished because of you?'

Just then Zere stepped out of the house and began cursing them vehemently. 'I don't know your laws nor your punishment system,' she yelled. 'All I know is that you are a bunch of brats and you keep bothering us. You do things that God would not approve of. Alla ma yekbela... God will not accept it. God is looking at you from high above and will settle the score on Judgement Day!'

'Be quiet, stupid woman,' yelled one of the boys. 'Your day will also come.'

Their father, who was home at the time, did not dare step outside. Neighbors, on the other hand, left their homes and began cursing the boys. Some of them even threw rocks at the gang, since the Christians had also suffered from them.

'This isn't over!' yelled the boy and waved his hands. 'We will return and get our revenge.' The three turned their donkeys around and departed.

That same year saw further attempts to remove Hisne from her parents' home. Some did it by requesting her hand, but some tried tricks - anything to get her away from Shmuel, who wouldn't leave her side.

Over the years I've heard many stories from my Aunt Hisne. I've heard stories from my father Shamca and my Aunt Sarah too. Some of them seemed so peculiar that I had difficulty believing they were true. Sometimes I would forget that I live in a different place, in a different time.

Some of those instances had to do with stories about the relationship between adult men and young boys and girls. These days when we hear stories of men chasing little girls, the word that comes to mind is pedophilia. It is defined as sexual deviance and characterized by a sexual attraction to children. It is considered a crime in all enlightened countries.

Yet in the Islamic worldview it is not considered deviance. This would be the right moment to mention that in Islam, having sexual relationships with young girls is not considered a crime and the Koran even encourages marriage to young girls. This Islamic-pedophilic practice originated in the days of the prophet Muhammad. After the death of his first wife Khadīja, he married eleven women and had multiple mistresses.

Muslim writings tell us that Muhammad would schedule visits to the tents of his wives according to their menstruation cycles. His sexual appetite was endless. In the book Sahih al-Bukhari, one of Islam's key texts, it is written that the prophet would visit his wives in rotation throughout the day and night, and that there were eleven of them. It was said that his sexual prowess was that of thirty men. In order to satisfy these needs he kept a "mistress stable", where the women were held against their will.

One of those women was Rihanna, the Jewess. According to Islamic law, Mohammad's wives and mistresses had no choice but to satisfy his sexual needs at any time, day and night. The texts mention that he enjoyed them from the top of the head to the toes. This was not seen as anything out of the ordinary for Muslims, not even in the case of Aisha, one of Muhammad's favorites.

Aisha was the daughter of Abu Bakr, a close friend and the most loyal admirer of the prophet. Later he would become the first caliph, following Muhammad's death. As soon as Muhammad noticed Aisha, he immediately began fantasizing about having intercourse with her. His fantasy would not have been seen as normal today - it was pure pedophilia, as Aisha was a little girl, only four or five years old, while the prophet was in his fifties. Muhammad wasted no time in turning his private fantasy into reality.

When Aisha turned six, Muhammad asked for her hand from her father. Abu Bakr thought this kind of relationship was inappropriate - not because Aisha was six but because he considered himself Muhammad's brother. The prophet immediately tore down his objection. As God's messenger on earth, he claimed that the union was right in the eyes of Allah. Abu Bakr believed, like all Muslims did, that the prophet was indeed speaking for God. He accepted his words and Muhammad married the girl.

After their marriage, Muhammad in his mercy allowed Aisha to bring her toys with her to their shared tent, including her dolls. The marriage was consummated when Aisha was nine years old, and Muhammad 53. The reason for this waiting period was not because Muhammad didn't want to sexually abuse a six-year-old, but because she fell ill and lost her hair.

Pedophilia in Islam went well beyond Muhammad. Unfortunately, it is allowed and supported by the Koran. For instance, in the debate over the appropriate waiting period for deciding whether or not a woman got pregnant before or after a divorce, the holy texts conclude that when in doubt about a wife whose

menstrual cycle has stopped - i.e. she's pregnant - the waiting period is three months. The same law was true for women who haven't yet had a period due to their young age. That meant a husband could not banish his wife until it was certain that it wasn't his child that she was carrying.

The Koran discusses child pregnancies as a normal occurrence. In other words it does not forbid pedophilia. Some might claim that Jewish sources cite marriage to young girls as well. This is mentioned in commentaries and various holy texts. My response to this is that while things were indeed so, hundreds of years ago, they were eventually abandoned and recognized as crimes. Not so with the Muslims, who never abandoned this horrific practice.

Surely everyone remembers how the Ayatollah Ruhollah Khomeini, the most famous Islamic religious figure of the 20th century, stated that a man can enjoy sexual pleasure from a girl and even a baby. The Ayatollah clarified that in both cases the man cannot penetrate, though sodomizing a boy is allowed; and that if a man penetrates a girl he must support her financially for the rest of his life, and she cannot be one of his four permanent wives. He further explained that the man could not also marry the girl's sister, and that in general, the girl is better off marrying so that she gets her first period in her husband's home rather than in her father's.

Sodomy in children was not rare among the non-Jewish community of Kurdistan. I remember my father telling my mother - whispering in Kurdish, so I wouldn't understand - that on at least two occasions, while walking the fields and collecting wood in Kurdistan, he ran into men sodomizing boys. Once, he heard the child crying, which didn't seem to deter the sodomizer or prevent him from continuing. My mother did not react, but by the look on her face I understood that she believed him. I, on the other hand, had a hard time believing.

Nor could I believe my father's descriptions of just how huge the Barzan caves were. He once told me that these caves could fit tens of thousands of people. Ten-thousand, twenty-thousand, maybe even fifty-thousand! As a child, I thought this sounded ridiculous and unrealistic. That's because as a child, I visited the caves of Jerusalem, which could fit a few dozen people at most. Only later, as an adult, I saw huge caves around the world, which could fit thousands. Today, I know that Barzan also had huge caves.

The reason I'm paralleling the cave story and the child abuse story is to explain that in both cases I thought my father was exaggerating and I didn't believe his words. Just like I'd never witnessed huge caves as a boy, I couldn't believe an adult could do such horrible things. Years later, reading a similar story in Sami Michael's book, Storm Among the Palms, I remembered my father's shocking stories and realized that he was speaking the truth.

The Jews in Kurdistan used to marry off their daughters early too, but no earlier than age 12, which is unthinkable today. In town, orphans were engaged even earlier, but only to prevent the Muslims from taking orphans and converting them against their will.

In those days when children lost their parents and needed assistance from family members, some didn't hesitate to sell them to Muslims. Being engaged at a young age ensured that no one else would ask for their hand in marriage, since engagements were listed in municipality and governments institutions.

The custom of converting children to Islam has been a popular practice since Islam's early days. To prevent this, organizations were set up to save children. In Akra, for instance, one of the town's leaders, Khwaja Khano, took orphans from all over the region into his home. Some of them were sent by their families. That's exactly where Zere sent her sister Chizeme after their parents died.

Hisne, who was tremendously beautiful, drew attention from many, and particularly from Muslims. "Living like that," she explained, "made life in Harran even more difficult. My mother was afraid I would be kidnapped and kept demanding we move to Akra, a place which left a good impression on her following the two weeks she spent there. 'I'm tired of always looking out for Hisne, chasing her around and watching her closely every time she goes out to the fields,' she would complain. Eventually my father realized there was no other choice but to move to Akra."

When we left Harran, our family had the same number of members as it did when we left Barzan," declared Hisne. "Mame and Aharon died and were buried in Harran, while Nergez - who was born in Bas, and little Mame - who was a newborn, made us five children again. The distance between Harran and Akra was two day's walk. We acquired very few items while living in Harran: we had a little bit of wool, strings and fabrics, as well as some kitchen utensils and clothing.

The family debated on how to walk to Akra. We wondered whether it would be better for father to arrived before us in order to ask his brother Moshe for a pair of donkeys "on loan", so that we could carry the few belongings we had. Alternatively, we thought perhaps it was better to begin the journey immediately, before any of the Muslims who threatened us attempted to make good on their threats and seek revenge. My father decided not to take the risk. His survival instinct was stronger than the will to hold on to our belongings.

We left immediately, though we did take the clothes, pots, and utensils that we could carry, with us. We wrapped them in bundles, bukche in Kurdish, loaded them on our backs and made our way toward Akra. Halfway between Harran and Akra is a place called Bira Capra. A few families lived there, but it was hardly a village - more like a roadside rest-stop. There was water, as implied by the name "Bira", meaning: well, and fruit trees.

But most important of all, the town had 'soft soil,' as Sarah put it, 'on which you can sleep comfortably.'

"True, very true," confirmed Hisne. "The soil was soft. But we weren't alone. There was another family or two, along with all their stuff, but we mostly saw merchants with their goods. After a light meal of bread and some fruit, we put our heads on the warm ground and fell into a deep sleep.

Akra, unlike the other places we lived, was a real city, with approximately 3,000 residents - one hundred of them, Jews. It was divided into neighborhoods, or "mahlat(s)", in Arabic. There was a Tostanaye mahlat, a Gugowa mahlat and a Ju mahlat - a Jewish neighborhood. That was the name given to it by the Muslims, and it probably came from the British use of the word Jew, during their rule.

Upon arriving at Akra, our family met us with mixed feelings. Some were glad we came, because this was a chance to bring the family back together. But some turned-up their noses, knowing that we had nothing to contribute to the family and that in financial terms, we would be a burden on Moshe and his family. Moshe didn't bother giving us a room near his home; we had to rent one a bit farther away and far from the Jewish neighborhood.

When we managed to save some money from our hard work in agriculture, we moved to a slightly closer room in the Jewish area. The room was so small that it couldn't fit all of us. Binyamin, Moshe's younger brother, lived with his brother in the same neighborhood. To be precise, only his wife and three daughters lived there; he worked in villages around town and lived in the nearby village of Sapti.

Binyamin's job was to escort brides, mostly Muslim - that was a real profession. He had to be a good horseman, as escorting the bride was a complex and special ceremony. In fact, it was a series of ceremonies that began with the henna ceremony. The original Kurdish henna ceremony took place in the bride's home. The sharply-dressed groom arrives on horseback, covered with flowers and accompanied by family members and a Kurdish orchestra with a drum and a flute called a davul-zurna.

Once the groom and his family arrive at the bride's house, they begin exchanging greetings and good wishes between the families, while the guests dance, sing and praise the new couple.

During the henna ceremony, the eldest of the tribe, usually a woman, places pieces of lokum (Turkish Delight) on the fingers of the bride and groom, which are eaten directly from their hands by the unmarried guests, as a charm for finding themselves a partner.

The henna is placed in the hands of the bride and groom, with the groom's right hand and the bride's left hand covered with a green kerchief, symbolizing abundance and fertility. Next is the giving of gifts, which is traditionally gold and silver jewelry. This is the cue to begin the real celebration, with a lot of food, singing and dancing.

On the day of the wedding, the bride mounts a horse wearing her wedding dress and the jewelry she received from the groom's family - her face covered. The horseman walks at the head of the convoy, which follows the bride. The convoy includes all the villagers, who escort the bride with music and dance. The horseman leads the bride to the groom's village, which was sometimes a few hour's walk. Throughout the journey, the villagers sing, dance and shoot their guns into the air.

The Jews had their henna ceremonies on Tuesdays. The women would gather in the morning to make delicacies for later that evening. The ceremony continued for two days: Tuesday and Wednesday. The wedding would take place on Thursday. Again, the women met early in the morning to prepare the food. The bride arrived on horseback wearing a colorful dress, usually in shades of red and pink, her head covered by colorful tulle.

Meanwhile, at the groom's house they set up a structure called a gnina - a sukkah or temporary hut, surrounded by barmal fabrics - beautiful colorful textiles woven by the men. In Kurdistan only the men weaved, while the women spun the yarn. The gnina (in some communities it was called a gnini) was also the bride and groom's private room. Here, the groom lifted the tulle from over his bride's face.

The guests would dance around the room, while the bride and groom were inside alone, usually for 15 or 20 minutes. The groom would hold the bride's hands and they would talk and get to know each other. When they left the gnina, the wedding ceremony began. The chuppah was held by four single men, a charm to help them marry soon. Right after the ceremony, the music and dancing began again and usually lasted through the middle of the night.

The next day, Friday, the women cooked again, this time for the "Shabbat Hatan" (groom's Sabbath). They made all sorts of dishes, including different types of kubbeh (hamusta, matfuniya,...). In the spring, they also made curry. Yaprakh was prepared from stuffed vine leaves and other stuffed vegetables such as onions, eggplant, zucchini, cabbage. Certain women were in charge of baking the bread - red bread or lakhma smoka, thin bread or lakhma rakika and tursu - pickled vegetables. Throughout these days, and particularly on the Sabbath, everyone danced to the sound of the davul-zurna. On Sabbath they went to temple. At the the conclusion of the prayers, the groom was escorted to his house with singing and dancing but no instruments, to respect the Sabbath's holiness. Everyone sang and danced, with one or two leading the way and the others following. As a bride escort, Binyamin came to Akra only on weekends, and not every week. In fact, Sapti was his home, just like it was for his nephews: Gado and Abd al Rahman."

Two years after arriving at Akra, Binyamin welcomed his first son, following three daughters. When his son turned four months old, Binyamin fell ill.

"Binyamin spoke to the angels," recalled Sarah. "When we visited him and sat by his bed, he would hallucinate and speak as if he was talking to the grim reaper. 'You will not take my soul until I see my entire family by my side,' he would say, to an invisible entity. 'I will not give you my soul until I see my brothers Moshe and David with their children, my wife, my daughters, and my six-month-old son Zechariah - whom I hardly had a chance to know...' And indeed, as we stood by his bed, he looked around at everyone, closed his eyes and told the angel of death, 'Now do what you want with me.'

Binyamin returned his soul to his creator. He was buried in Akra. His wife and children continued living there, but moved to another room nearer Moshe and cleared their old room out for us.

And so we went to live on the slope of the Jewish neighborhood, above Moshe's house, with his roof as our yard. Elo, who journeyed with us from Barzan with his two children, moved into another room nearby."

Hisne listened closely and added more details from her memory. "Moshe arrived at Akra three years before we did. Since he had not succeeded in selling his fields and orchards in Barzan, he left all his belongings behind. The locals, who knew he had no choice but to leave, wouldn't pay him a single cent.

Thankfully, Moshe had a lot of money. He traded it in for golden coins - gold lira. He kept the coins in fabric or leather bags tied with string. It was a worldwide Jewish custom to trade belongings for gold and diamonds. These were easier to carry and easy to trade wherever one went.

With his money, Moshe bought a fine home in Akra and a few animals such as goats, chickens and donkeys.

He stopped working in agriculture entirely, and most of his living was made from trading animals. As in many other homes, he had a small vegetable garden in a corner of his house.

Most households in Akra grew vegetables inside the house, since there were no floors. One corner would be used as a vegetable garden to grow mostly onions and radishes. But in Moshe's house, there was never a shortage of food. His friend, Mustafa Barzani, who had promised to send him crops a few times a year, kept his promise.

My parents on the other hand, found it very difficult to make a living in Akra. My father began weaving again, a skill shared by his brother Moshe, except Moshe did not rely on it for income. Weaving was considered a man's work in Kurdistan but unfortunately, the trousers that my father made were not fashionable in Akra. Merchants in Akra, which was near Erbil, a large county city with over fifty-thousand residents, bought their clothes in the big city.

People had no interest in the goods my father was making. Since he could not make anything else, and did not want to work in the field, he insisted on making the trousers and going to small villages to try and sell them. Occasionally, he would take Sarah along. She was nine-years-old and he preferred taking her, since she was lightweight and very obedient. He did not get along with Shamca, who was impatient and liked to argue, and according to my father, walked too quickly. Sarah and my father would fold the fabrics, place them on a blanket, tie the four ends together - a bukche - place it on their backs, and leave. Sarah told us there was no demand at all for these fabrics. If anyone made a purchase, it was out of pity, not need. They would pay him in mere cents, dirhams.

My mother was the one who took care of food. Despite all of our hardships, she never neglected the rules of kashrut. She would fill the pots that she brought from Harjawa, a Christian village near Akrawhich, with water, and boil it for an entire hour - just to make them kosher, like we do before Passover. She worked very hard in her agricultural work. She, Shmuel and I - and sometimes Sarah when she wasn't busy working with our father - would work in the area villages, including Harjawa, which had rice fields.

Not far from Akra was a village named Bijil. Its residents were rich and filled high positions in the government. Bijil had a waterfall which provided water for the rice fields of the local rich. I've never seen water as clear and clean, transparent and delicious, as the waterfall in Bijil. We used to drink the water, wash our faces, and dip our feet in it. It was one of the few pleasures we had back then. That waterfall gave us moments of grace, which were not frequent in Kurdistan.

The villagers' relationship with the Jews was excellent. We worked their fields as well as the fields of Harjawa. The rice harvest took place in summer, in peak heat. We worked the fields with water reaching our knees. We carried baskets on our backs. The rice stalks that we harvested with our hands, we would put in the baskets on our backs.

The heat was unbearable and we didn't have any food; the field owner never promised us food. As payment for our work, he gave us a few dirhams and some rice. The fields also hid many snakes. They lurked in the water, coiled around themselves. We walked between them as carefully as possible. We were told that the snakes did not bite and were not poisonous, but to be honest, I'm not sure that was true. Either way we had to be careful. Once, as we were walking in the field with the supervisor next to us, I felt that the basket on my back was heavier than usual. Suddenly I heard the supervisor's rolling laughter. 'Why are you laughing?' I asked him, but he just kept laughing. I remembered that one of the stalk

piles had felt heavier than the others when I picked it up. The supervisor saw that it contained a snake, causing the increased weight. His rolling laughter aroused my suspicion. I took the basket off my back and looked - and indeed, I saw the snake. I yelled at the supervisor in anger. 'Why did you laugh instead of warning me?' He continued laughing and replied that the snake wouldn't do me any harm. 'What are you so worried about?' he asked and kept laughing.

At the end of the day we finished our work, received payment, and returned home. On the way, I told my mother that I no longer wanted to work at picking rice. She smiled and replied, 'We survived the Barzan bombings, we survived the Harran hell, and now, when we're finally doing okay and getting paid, you break down because of a snake? Can a snake really bring us down?' She gave me a big smile and added, 'God Almighty loves us. Don't worry. He's with us and I always feel it.'

Akra was a small town. The distance from the battlefields - which were mostly around Barzan - made it safe. On the other hand, its proximity to big cities like Mosul and Erbil made it a perfect haven for those who had a reason to escape.

"One day a young man arrived at Akra - the most beautiful man I've ever seen," recalled Sarah with a smile. "How old am I today? 86? I've not seen a boy so beautiful since then," she stated, then added secretively, "They said he murdered another man, in another city, for romantic reasons...yet another battle over a woman's heart."

At this point, it is worth mentioning that no law existed regarding such cases. At the time, Kurdistan did not belong to a country and the Iraqi government was yet to begin enforcing its laws on the Kurdish region in the north of the state. There were unwritten laws known as urf, from the Arabic root "aref" meaning, to know. Urf means something akin to, it is known that... It was indeed known that a man who murdered someone was destined to be revenged.

"That same man who arrived to Akra fearing revenge was also seeking work," continued Sarah. "He approached the field owners and asked whether they needed workers. This was during a very hot summer, during harvest season. He got a job working in a field which was a two hour walk from Akra, maybe even farther. His job was to cut the crops with a scythe. Other workers followed him, picked up the sheaves and arranging them in piles. We were working for the same owner, also picking up crops from the field.

One day, the field owner came to us and asked that we accompany the man for a few days, while he harvested. So, we followed him: my mother, Shmuel, Hisne and I. We were joined by our neighbor, a single man about 30 years old named Beno, who was my mother's cousin.

We arrived at the field. The harvester, who was tall and muscular, with blue eyes and a large red kerchief around his head, began working.
I don't remember whether he spoke, whether he told us what to do, or guided us. That's how much I was charmed by his beauty. Interesting, I really don't recall if he said anything. Remember, I was only nine-and-a-half years old. Shmuel was 12 and Hisne 13. The five of us were supposed to put the sheaves into piles. The work was hard and the heat unbearable. This man worked very fast; we could hardly keep up with him.
Occasionally we took short breaks to drink the water we brought along with us in a leather pouch. The water was so warm that it was hardly fit for drinking, even though we placed the pouch under a pile of crops.
When evening came, he ordered us to cease working. 'That's it, we're done for the day,' he said. 'We'll continue tomorrow.' We decided to spend the night in the field rather than walk the two hours home and return the next day, walking another two hours. Even if we went home, we would have to sleep on the ground since we didn't have any beds. And the soil in the field was softer than at home. In the blazing heat, sleeping outside was the best option.
When darkness fell we began to feel hungry. My mother ordered me to go home, bake bread and return so that we could eat before going to sleep. Beno offered to go with me, since it was not a good idea for a nine-year-old girl to walk such a long and desolate road on her own. The two of us, Beno and I, left for Akra.
We arrived after two hours. Beno, who was living with his parents in the same neighborhood, went home. I also went home, and began baking. I took water and flour, made dough, lit the fire and placed the saj on top. I baked the bread. When it was done, I took the entire loaf, which was thin and round, and arranged it in one big pile. The whole process took about an hour. I loaded

the bread on my back and went to Beno's house. He brought along some bread that his mother had baked and we made our way to the field.

When we arrived, no one was there. I knew for certain that this was the right place - I knew the road well, and Beno was with me. I panicked. Thoughts began racing in my head. I knew the beautiful man was a murderer - he seemed pleasant and polite, but he did kill someone not so long ago. I couldn't stop thinking about it. Who knows? Maybe he lusted after beautiful Hisne, killed my mother and my brother, and kidnapped her!

I began shouting with all my might: 'Dayke, dayke...' meaning: mother, in Kurmanji. 'Calm down,' said Beno. I ignored him and screamed even harder. 'Dayke...! Shmuel...! Hisne...!' I'm not sure how long it had been since our arrival. Perhaps half-an-hour, perhaps more, still my shouts went unanswered. 'Shhh, silence,' Beno suddenly whispered. 'Shhh...' We went quiet. From far away we heard dogs barking. We knew that where there were dogs, there were also houses. Arabs kept dogs in their yard to protect them from foxes, jackals and unwanted human visitors.

We began walking toward the sounds. After half-an-hour's walk or so, we saw dim lights in the distance. No electricity was available then, of course. The lights could have been fanuzes - oil or kerosene lamps with a wick sticking out of them, or bonfires, we couldn't tell for sure. We continued walking toward them. Suddenly we saw human figures walking toward us. I recognized my mother's walk, along with Shmuel, Hisne and the stranger. I breathed deep, relieved, and wiped away the tears so that my mother wouldn't notice that I had been crying.

As they neared, I noticed my mother was carrying something on her back. 'Where were you?' I cried. 'Right here, my darling,' she answered. 'We went to someone's yard, snuck in and grabbed a few onions.' And indeed

I saw that what she had on her back were fresh green onions, just pulled from the ground, still covered in dirt. We returned to the field, peeled the onions and enjoyed a feast of onions and lafa (taboon bread) with some hot water from the leather pouch. Our stomachs full, we went to sleep.

The next morning we awoke before sunrise, full of mosquito bites. We were so tired the night before that we hadn't noticed that mosquitos filled the air. We were bitten despite the fact that we tried to cover ourselves as best we could, with whatever clothes we had. Our headdress, called poshiya, did little to help. It was about a meter wide and a meter long and could cover either the head or the legs, but not both. We opted to cover our heads, but that meant that our feet were swollen with bites.

The beautiful man, who I'd wrongfully suspected of killing my mother and brother and kidnapping Hisne, ordered us to start working. We worked for a few more days, until we were done harvesting that field. We were paid with rice and wheat. I never saw any money exchange hands. It is possible that they paid my mother some money, perhaps a few dirhams, but I will never know for sure."

That same event was similarly engraved in Hisne's memory, particularly the return home and their meeting with their father. "When we arrived back to Akra, my father was sitting by the loom, weaving fabrics for trousers," she told me. "Before we even had a chance to step inside, he got up from his seat, turned to my mother and asked for the money. 'We didn't get any money,' she replied. 'We only got rice and wheat. Here it is, in front of you.'
'That's impossible,' my father said. 'Where is the money? Give it to me right now.' My mother, who knew exactly what would happen to her, quickly took out the few dirhams she had received and handed them over.
Sarah was much closer to my father than I was. She was his favorite daughter, partly because she was much more like him and also because she was too young to find herself other work. That's why they had their own special bond. She was agile and he found it easy to pass through villages with her.

After Sarah told him about the night she thought we were lost, he began to realize the severity of the situation. He knew that many had tried to have me for themselves and he feared someone might try and kidnap me. He also knew that if he didn't hurry up and get me engaged, he might not win the "bridewealth" he so desired.
My father quickly got up and went to his brother Moshe, to tell him what had happened. When Moshe heard the story, he decided to follow through on an idea he first came up with in Barzan: to arrange an engagement between Sarah, Binyamin's daughter, and his own son Barkuna. They were both 12-and-a-half. I was thirteen at the time and he destined me for his other son, Grib, who was two years younger than me.
Marrying off cousins was very acceptable back then. Today it's not so acceptable, mostly because of the

genetic risk of it. But in those days in Kurdistan there wasn't much of a choice. There were not many Jews in the villages and marrying Christians or Muslims was out of the question, so arranging marriages between cousins was acceptable and even desirable. After all, that was exactly what our forefathers did. Abraham married his son Isaac to his cousin Rivka, while she sent Yaakov to her brother Lavan's daughters. It wouldn't be an exaggeration to say that marrying cousins was even a mitzvah.

Moshe's notion of marrying Barkuna, his older son, to Sarah, was born of the fact that Barkuna was smarter and more settled than his brother and more like Moshe in character; he was savvy and witty. Moshe thought that Sarah would fit him well as she was also very clever. Grib, on the other hand, needed more guidance and protection. He was an introvert and depended greatly on his brother. That's why Moshe wanted him to marry Hisne, who was two years older than he was - so she could take him under her wing.

"Moshe and Binyamin talked it over and decided to marry Sarah and Barkuna," recalled Hisne. "Moshe paid half his due bridewealth, as was customary, with the other half to be paid at the wedding. Sarah agreed to the engagement and the date was set. However, when he turned to my father to express his wish to marry me to Grib, I refused and made a terrible fuss, even though my father gave his blessing. He saw it as a great opportunity for survival - with the money he would have received for my hand he could have lived a long time without working.

'You want me to marry such a young boy?' I screamed. I was 13 and Grib was 11. My family didn't really care for that side of the family, and we were not at all connected. We always saw them as patronizing and rich. Wherever we went - Sarah, Shamca and I - we always met with other friends or went on our own. Never with them.

Grib did like Shamca and wanted to meet us, but he was very dependent on his brother, who did not like us at all. That meant that Grib would often walk around in the fields on his own. It helped him develop a great sense of direction. When my father heard my refusal, he immediately reported it to Moshe. Not an hour passed before the two of them showed up at the doorstep. They walked over to me, raging, and together with my mother sat me on the floor. Moshe and my mother held me tight as my father brought the scythe and, in fury, said to me: 'Either agree to the engagement or I'll cut your head off...' Shamca, who saw the whole thing happen, would remember it for the rest of his days. He tensed, and instinctively began moving towards us, but then stopped and returned to his seat. Even mother...? he thought to himself. He gave another quick glance at the stick he used to carry around, which was now lying in the corner. But what if... he pondered. 'Could a son beat his mother and father?' In all honesty, there were many times before when he had really wanted to smack his own father. Now he was confused and helpless. How could mother be on his side? Did she forget what happened to her when she was younger? Shamca stuck to his spot. Perhaps he understood subconsciously that he shouldn't intervene.

'Something inside told me to stay out of it,' Shamca told me many years after the event took place. 'It just seemed like that's how things worked back then.'

"In this situation, having no other choice, with the scythe on my neck, I stuttered my consent," remembered Hisne. "That same awful event, when my mother was beaten to her core for her refusal to marry her sister, came up in my memory. In those days an engagement was considered half a marriage, at least. Apart from the consent of the two families, the hand shaking and bridewealth payment, the two families also signed an official document which approved the engagement

agreement and was entrusted to state institutions. The government representative was the Bureau of the Population Registry with branches in all county cities. The signed document was kept in the municipality building, which served as that county's branch of the Ministry of the Interior. From that moment on, I was engaged: married yet unmarried to an 11-year-old boy. No one could ask for my hand anymore. Worse than that, I wasn't even allowed to leave town without that boy's permission."

And so we spent two more years in Akra. We worked hard at any job we could get. We reaped wheat, weaved, worked the rice fields, did everything we could. As hard as Sarah, my mother and I worked, Shamca worked seven times as hard. He would stack on his back huge piles of wood and hurry to set them down so he could get another round. When we went to the fields with him he protected and supported us. When he was farther along, we would call to him to slow down. Many times, hearing our calls would cause him to walk even faster - as if to make us run. I used to ask Sarah not to call him so that he wouldn't get farther away from us.
In truth, beyond the will and need to stay together, our attempt to keep him in our sight (or at least a scream away) was also an important way for us to look out for Shamca, whose enthusiasm and speed sometimes turned into irresponsible actions.

The heavy loads we used to carry did not stop us from doing other things. If we needed to pick fruit, we would climb the tree with the loads tied to our backs. If we needed to drink from a natural water source on the road, we would bend over with the loads, reach for the water and sip like animals. Sometimes the water was in pits and warmed up with the sun. We couldn't care less: we just drank it warm. Nor did we care that other animals drank before us. We were often surrounded by snakes and other poisonous creatures. That didn't bother us either; we had no choice but to drink to survive.
One time, Shamca managed to get really far away from us. None of our calls were answered. We yelled and yelled - nothing. I had a bad feeling. Although he would often hear us and not answer, a game for him, this time I felt like something wasn't right. Even Sarah, who was stronger and faster than me and always a few steps ahead, was walking next to me that day. Perhaps she had a bad feeling about it too.

Suddenly she stopped, looked at me and asked, 'What's wrong, khalnti?' meaning: sister. 'What's wrong with me?' I asked. 'The question is, what's wrong with him!' We started walking faster. After a few minutes we saw a small grove in the distance. We ran over and saw Shamca hanging from one of the trees. As we came near, we saw that the wood load on his back had gotten caught up in the tree branches when he was climbing up to pick nuts.

Shamca was hanging by a thread. We stood underneath him to catch him, should he fall. 'Move over!' he yelled at us. 'I'll be fine.'

I got angry. 'How exactly?' I asked. 'Why didn't you call us? Why didn't you scream?' I knew that his ego wouldn't allow him to ask for any help. But all three of us also knew he couldn't fall this distance and remain unharmed.

During those days and where we were living, it was hard to heal from even the simplest of fractures. We saw horrible disabilities around us, often created by relatively mild injuries. Lacking proper medical care, any injury could be fatal. In a godforsaken place such as ours, no one knew how to cast bones or treat infections. Many remained disabled for the rest of their lives or died from gangrene or infection simply because no one knew how to help them.

We knew we couldn't let Shamca fall. We stood beneath him and refused to leave. Shamca, who was athletic and flexible, tried to lift himself up and grab a branch with his feet, but to no avail. Every time he made a movement, and the branch he was hanging from swayed, we screamed. I suggested he loosen the rope that was holding the wood to his back, but he had other plans. He began swinging forcefully on the branch, up and down, in order to break it. I thought this was a mistake - if the branch were to break, Shamca would fall four or five meters.

After swinging for a few minutes without breaking the branch, Shamca decided to try and loosen the rope and get one hand out. It took a lot of work but he finally managed to do so, and remained hanging only from his right shoulder. Now he began swinging again, holding the branch he was hanging from with his left hand. This was much easier. He lifted himself up and placed his left foot on the branch. Lying on the branch, with his right shoulder still tied, he held on to it with his legs, as tightly as he could. With his left hand he began untying his right hand. After freeing himself, he crawled on the branch like a skilled monkey, and slowly descended.
'Stop running away from us all the time,' I scolded him. 'We have to remain together at all times.'
He looked at me and said, 'I can't walk at your pace. It drives me crazy, walking so slowly. Don't worry, I'll always be a shout away, I can hear you always.'
We began our way back home. Once again, Shamca was walking in front and the two of us were trailing behind him. 'He just doesn't learn,' said Sarah. 'True,' I replied, 'but at least he managed to free himself and save face.' We both laughed and walked faster. We didn't often have many reasons to laugh, or even smile. None of our hard work brought in any income, neither in money nor in produce. We were hungry day and night with no livelihood to be found.
After Mame was born we had another mouth to feed. The money my father received for my engagement never left his hands - my mother, my sister, my brother and I did not see a single cent. The few gold lira that my father possessed, he hid well, usually in his clothes. The year Mame turned four was not a particularly tough winter. The snow that came down on the mountains was high, but in Akra, which was at the foothills, there was far less snow - only half-a-meter high. The children would go out to play, Mame too. Once while playing, she scooped up some snow, grabbed the edges of her dress,

and filled it with the snow. When the dress became entirely wet, the harsh cold got to her.

She ran into the yard, which was cleared of snow by then. In the middle of the yard a fire was burning. Mame stepped close to it in order to warm herself and dry her dress. Suddenly her dress caught fire, turning into a torch within seconds. The children began screaming loudly. One of them ran to call our mother, who came running, rolled Mame along the floor and put the fire out. Mame's yells were so loud that they brought all the neighbors out of their homes. She had burns on her legs, stomach and neck. My father, who also came running, lifted her in his arms and ran with her to Mualem Chucha, who was known for his abilities to cure almost any illness. He took a look at her and told my father he would take her in, but the treatment would take a few days. He ordered my father to wait 'til he returned with the medical herbs.

A few minutes later he came back with a big bundle of leaves. He ground them in the alcove used for threshing wheat. Then hewith his alcove, scrambled an egg with his finger, and spread the egg and leaf mixture onto Mame's burnt flesh. 'That's all,' he told my father. 'Now come back to me every day and bring a chicken with you - that will be my payment.' My father took Mame to him every other day to save on chickens. When I think of it today, I honestly couldn't say where my father found so many chickens to give to Mualem Chucha. It must have been very expensive. But two weeks later, having paid some 10 chickens, Mame's skin was all better.

That same year, my mother tried to have another son, so that Shmuel wouldn't be the only one. 'You need to stop working so hard if you want a baby boy,' the self-appointed "specialists" advised her. Back then everyone believed that hard work and carrying loads brought baby girls. My mother slowed down with her work, and yet, wouldn't you know - a girl was born after all. My mother named her Ruhama.

At the same time Ruhama was born, my brother fell ill with dysentery. He was feverish and weak, and began hallucinating, finally losing consciousness. His condition was so bad that at one point he couldn't control his own defecations. My mother and I sat by his bed long days and nights, applying damp cloths to his forehead and trying to get him to drink. Since he had so few clothes, Sarah and I had to wash them every day. The only water source was the spring, which was quite far from the village. Every time I went there, Muslims would harass me or attempt to kidnap me; I was in constant fear of them. My mother made me wash the clothes at night.

One night, while going to wash the clothes by myself, a man arrived on a horse. When he noticed me he asked, 'Are we all out of Muslims who can harm you? Why do you come here alone? Aren't you afraid of them? Don't you know they pass by here at night?' I was 14 at the time.

'God above is looking after me,' I replied. 'Even if the Muslims don't fear me, surely they fear God.' The stranger looked at me. 'Be careful, foolish girl,' he said and rode his horse away.

Upon returning home, I told my mother about that meeting. She was horrified. 'We can't even go to the spring at night anymore? What's left?' she asked. I didn't answer. 'Don't go alone anymore,' she ordered. 'Starting tomorrow, I'll do it myself.' Luckily, three weeks later Shmuel was better. Mualem Chucha attributed it to Shamca's physical strength, which helped the prayers.

Two years later my sister Nergez fell ill with rubella. Today it is considered an easy illness to treat, but back then - 70- or 80- years ago - everything was much more complex. Perhaps it also had to do with neglect on my parents' side. Our financial state was so bleak that we

had no time to look after Nergez. Many children died from rubella in Barzan - it really was a godforsaken place, high up in the mountains. But in Akra, a town of 2,000-3,000 people and a two hour ride from Mosul and Erbil, there must have been more options than turning to Mualem Chucha or depending on God's good graces. Within a few weeks, Nergez passed away and was buried in Akra's cemetery. It all happened so fast that I can't even recall a funeral or sitting shiva. We simply continued with our lives. The hunger, that pesky and burdening hunger, was the only thing we cared about.

The fields we knew well, even the farthest ones, were the ones that gave us life. The wild fields, which belonged to no one, were full of fruit trees, weeds and plants. The abundance of water meant that the fields were green and fruitful all year-round. We knew the flora well. We knew the effects of the seasons and when each tree yielded fruit and which were fit for eating.

In order to avoid picking fruit in the heat, we went to the fields in the evening, before it got dark. Sometimes the journey would take two or three hours of walking. Picking fruit early in the morning had its benefits. The fruit tasted better when it was cold, still soaked in morning dew.

Upon arrival, we would go inside one of the area caves. We knew the environment like the palm of our hand. We would spent the night in the cave and early in the morning, before dawn, we would go out to the field and begin picking. We had an advantage over other pickers in that we worked as a team. Shamca, who was tall, got to the higher branches with the best fruit. He would bend the branches so that we could pick the fruit. We knew when each fruit matured and when was the best time was to pick it.

But we knew much more than just the trees and the plants. We lived in nature. The caves we slept in were not protected from wolves and jackals, or gurga. The wolves were the animals we feared the most, especially when they appeared in packs of three or four, and even more. Sometimes we found a single wolf in the cave, sometimes a pair, but in a pack - that's when they were the most dangerous. We would light fires in the cave, both in order to see and in order to scare the wolves away.

"One night, we met up a group of ten Jewish youths," Hisne recalled. "me, Shamca, Sarah, and a few friends. We enjoyed meeting in groups and going to the fields.

We would sit in one of the caves, tell stories, and sing together. I had a beautiful singing voice - I think I've already told you how I would sing at Barzan weddings. That night I was six or seven years old. My cousin Sarah was there too. When the stories and songs ended we fell asleep in the cave, warmed by the cosy fire. It was a very cold night. One of the boys even said he could smell the snow. It was an expression our parents would often use - 'Rikh talga le', meaning: I smell snow. When one of the elders said it, it meant that snow would begin falling the following day. And indeed, when we awoke the next morning, the fields were covered with snow about a meter deep.

We couldn't walk around and we couldn't return home. Luckily, we gathered enough wood to light a fire so we could stay there the whole day, as well as the next night. When we again stepped out the following morning, we discovered that the snow had remained the same height. It's true that the sky was already brighter and the sun had come out, and throughout the day the snow began slowly melting - but it was still not possible to walk through.

We sat around the fire, wondering whether we should try to make our way in the snow with the wood that we still had, or stay another day while the sun melted the snow. We had another problem which was much more critical: the food that we had taken with us the first day, was running out. We knew that another day without food would be very hard. The boys were all for leaving the cave. They believed we could clear our way with the sticks and make our way home.

In my experience, men find it more difficult than women to endure hunger. That was true in Kurdistan and equally true in Israel and anywhere else in the world. We hadn't brought a lot of food with us. My mother had given each of us two lakhma rakika, a thin bread baked on the saj. My mother would spread tahini over the bread - about half a meter in diameter - and fold it in a special way as so to keep the tahini from dripping. To do the folding, my mother would take two edges and fold each one up to the middle. Then she would take the bottom and top edges and fold a quarter way. The result is a rectangle with tahini 'locked' inside. She then folded the rectangle in half and created a well-sealed square.

That day, she gave us each two of these - but we ate them both the first evening. We never imagined we would have to stay there more than one day. Now that two whole days had passed without having anything to eat, we had no choice but to leave the cave, with Shamca leading the way. He began clearing the snow and making progress. The distance from home was a two-hour walk, assuming the road was clear and dry. Shamca cleared the snow and went up the hill, one step at a time. Sarah followed. She was light and quick, while I was heavier and a little clumsy. I was 17, Shamca was 16 and Sarah was 14 1/2.

Of the three of us, I was the least fit. I wasn't entirely out-of-shape, but my brother and sister were better built and in excellent shape. After a few hundred meters, Sarah noticed I was having trouble walking. She slowed down and walked next to me. Shamca didn't slow down. He climbed up the hill, stopping occasionally to glance backwards and shout 'Ana zli!' meaning: 'I'm out of here'. A few hundred meters more and we couldn't even see him anymore, though we did maintain a 'shouting distance', as usual.

The journey was very difficult. It was freezing and we had no shoes. Our legs were wrapped in rags, leftover fabrics from my father's work. We tied them with strings. Sometimes we would add a small amount of straw, which made the walk easier and maintained the temperature, though the snow froze our legs.

The pain was almost too much to take. It felt like if I were to hit one of my toes, even carefully, it would fall off. The pain was so sharp that it reached our brains and our hearts. I could feel it inside my eyes.

Not far from where the road diverged, was a spring with water that was much warmer than the ground temperature. It wasn't a hot-water spring, as it was only two or three degrees celsius, but compared to the environment, submerging our cold feet felt warm. Sarah and I decided to walk over to it in order to ease the pain. We called Shamca to let him know. 'Fine, fine,' he said impatiently.
We turned from the road and headed toward the spring, which was only a short walk away. We cleared the snow from the rocks, sat down, and dipped our feet in the water. It felt supreme. The warmth spread through our bodies and eased the sharp pain in our feet.
"Meanwhile, Shamca arrived at the house. When my mother saw him enter alone she worried about our whereabouts. 'They went to the spring,' Shamca told her. 'They must be so cold,' she said and began crying. 'I should go fetch them.' But Shamca told her there was no need, 'They know their way back. They'll get here by themselves.'
It was late afternoon before we arrived home, aching all over. Our mother hugged us, helped us out of our wet clothes, and sat us by the open fire. She poured us some hitte dike, a warm and heavy stew. It was a delicious dish that we both loved. Eating it after long hours of hunger in the freezing cold, was sheer delight.
The hitte dike is a winter stew, one of the most beloved dishes in Kurdistan. It was usually eaten on the Sabbath. Preparing it was a ritual that began before the Sabbath and continued to the end.
The stew was made from wheat grains, which were ground until the chaff was removed, and dried leg

of cow or goat. In addition, kubbeh balls with a large amount of kaliya was added.

My mother would make it on Friday, before the Sabbath would commence. Then she would dig a pit in the ground, about 40 cm deep, and fill it with palle - burning coals. She would place the pot on the coals and seal it with mud and dirt. This ensured that the pot received all the heat. Perhaps she did leave a small opening to let oxygen in.

The ground around the pot was very warm. The pot, which was covered with fabric - dublabe - released a pleasant warmth and a wonderful smell. Once the Sabbath began, we sat on the floor, around the pot, with our feet near the pot. All Sabbath we would tell stories, argue, and sometimes laugh. At night we slept there, our feet warmed by the fire.

Kurdistan was freezing cold, particularly during the long winter nights. We only left the warmth of the pot for a few minutes, in order to use the toilet or anything else that was absolutely necessary - otherwise we might freeze to death.

We told each other different and diverse stories. Today it might be hard to imagine entire families sitting around one pot and telling stories. But back then, with no electricity, no radio, certainly no television, and with long, cold winter nights, all we could do was share stories. Winter nights were particularly dark because of the heavy clouds that covered the moon. Snowy nights also had strong winds.

As in many other cultures, some truly hair-raising stories were told of ghosts, witches and other strange creatures looking to harm human beings. Some told the stories so well that we could swear we had seen these creatures with our very own eyes.
Like the trolls of Scandinavia, born in long winter nights: vampire stories in Transylvania, Romania: elves in the Alps: and more, we in Kurdistan had herche and hambalulka.
Herche was a demon. Sometimes she would come to people in the middle of the night and start screaming between their tents so loudly it would make their blood run cold. 'Come and see, see what has happened in the forest...' she would yell. Suddenly she would start running toward the forest and everyone following. When she lured people deep into the forest, she placed a spell over them and made them dance in ecstasy; while they danced she would choke them to death. Only those who managed to wake from the ecstasy could escape; the rest would suffocate. Many people in Kurdistan would swear on their lives that - thanks to God - they awoke from their ecstasy at the very last minute and were saved.
"Today there are no such things as demons," explained Hisne. "Today we know so much... We can read and write, we have cars and computers. The demons must have run away, they no longer have room in modern society."

I looked at her and smiled. "Believe me," she added, "there really were demons. If my parents told me about them, they must have known what they were talking about. Elo told us about them too - and he never lied."

They also had many stories of cemeteries and the dead. "Let me tell you about something that once happened in my family," said Hisnie, smiling as if she was keeping a secret. "My grandmother Hisne, for whom I'm named, had a sister. She died and was buried in the cemetery in Barzan. Four days after her burial, people walked by and heard voices from the cemetery. When they neared her grave they saw the ground move. You know, in Kurdistan they didn't place stones on graves. So they bent over and heard my grandmother's sister calling from the ground: 'I'm not dead! Why did you bury me?' They immediately began digging, and managed to pull her out. She was as white as the snow. After she recovered, she told her shocked saviors: 'I was there, in the other world... They told me that if I want to keep on living I can't expose myself to the sun. I'm old and I don't move too well, but I do want to live... Please don't leave me in the sun!' At first they thought she was hallucinating and paid little attention to her words. But after a week of staying in the sun, she died - this time for good.

We had many stories of that sort. And by the way, a cemetery in Arabic is called a maqbara, which is believed to be the source for the word 'macabre' in many languages. Well, in Kurdistan we had plenty of macabre tales too."

Another popular type of story was variations on biblical tales. One of the most popular was the story of King Solomon and the demons. Solomon had a thousand wives and he spoke all the world's languages, including the language of animals. One day, he summoned 500 demons and ordered them to look for the 500 most beautiful virgins in the world. Each was instructed to

travel the world on his own, and bring back one virgin. They were to bring them to King Solomon so he could check their beauty - and their chastity. The demons traveled the entire world looking for the virgins but by the time they found them and came back, Solomon had died. What could they have possibly done? They married their virgins and the first Kurdish people were born...
This was a Kurdish legend that was created to tell about Kurdish characteristics: that they were beautiful on the one hand, but the sons and daughters of demons, on the other hand."
Listening to Hisne tell the story - or any other story for that matter - in her rich Kurdish is pure joy. Her whole face lights up and she fascinates her listeners with her magical descriptions.

"One day, my uncle Moshe suddenly became very ill with an illness that I didn't recognize," Hisne remembered. "Looking back, I think it must have been diabetes because he became very bloated and red, especially in his face. Gradually he weakened and lost control, until he couldn't even stand up straight. His sons set up a dudya for him - that's a hammock in Kurdish - which was made from wood boards and leather, tied between two trees; they would push it and let him swing.

I remember him spending a lot of time in that hammock. Only when someone came over to help him swing, did his pain subside a little bit. Once he called me over to him. 'Hisne, you know that I love you more than I do my own children,' he said quietly. 'You know that even back in Barzan I liked you and appreciated you very much, especially when I saw how well you take care of the other children and keep them busy. I will die soon, Hisne...'
'Don't say that,' I interrupted. He hushed me and went on. 'Today you are engaged to my son Grib. I don't trust my sons all that much. After I'm gone, I want you to guide them the right way. Use your wisdom. I've hidden some money both inside and outside the house. There is gold lira under the sitta, the stone we use for grinding. There is also money inside the house and money in the ceiling...' He told me exactly where to find the money.
Moshe spent a few more days in the hammock, swinging with the help of his sons. One day I walked over to him and noticed he was lifeless. I began screaming for Grib and Barkuna to come over. 'How do you know he's dead?' they yelled from afar. 'Come here and see for yourselves!' I answered. The walked over and saw that their father had indeed passed away.
Even though Moshe's death was to be expected, we were all very moved. He was not only the head of the

family but also a man who was respected wherever he went, even by Muslims. He was respected for his riches as well as for his serious appearance. Some people are born with a sort of halo over their heads. We can't see it or define it, but it does make us respect them all that much more. It must be some combination of their appearance, character, behavior and more. Combined, all these create a man who is different, somehow slightly better than the rest... such was Moshe.

After his passing, we called on his two older sons, Abd al Rahman and Gado, who were living in Sapti, to return home. Moshe was buried in Akra, alongside the grave of my sister Nergez. Following his death, an awkward situation was created in the family. Moshe was the leader - it was thanks to the respect he received from Muslims that we were never harassed or bothered. Now that he had died, we felt our security vanish. This wasn't only a feeling; it had manifested in our daily lives.

One day I was sitting on the roof, spinning yarns in the tashiya. My sister Mame, now seven, was by my side. We used to drop the strings to the floor and twist them into shape. While spinning the tashiya, I hadn't noticed that someone had cut the string.

'Who is the son-of-a-bitch-dog who cut my string?' I shouted in rage.

'Show your face and see for youself,' a voice answered from under the roof. I thought I recognized it, but I didn't answer. 'I'm waiting,' he called again, 'come see for yourself.' I asked Mame to peek over the low fence bordered the roof. 'Not you,' said the voice. 'It's not your face I want to see... Tell your sister to peek.'

At this point my doubts vanished. I recognized the voice and knew to whom it belonged. I asked Mame to climb down and fetch my father. When he arrived he said, 'It's the Sheikh's son. We don't want to mess with him. Stay here for the night. I'll stay by your side and we'll wait for him to leave.' All night long we stayed on the roof, even though he had already left. Not until dawn did we come down.

With our new situation there really was no point in staying in Akra anymore. All I could do was get married - thus stopping the harassments - or leave Akra for Baghdad. After mourning for Moshe for seven days I told Grib that before Moshe's death he told me where his money was hidden. I also told him that Moshe's final request of me was that I guard the money as well as his boys.

'The gold is in three different locations,' I said to Grib and told him the three hiding places. 'Don't tell anyone, so that we can take the money and give our family a good starting point. Grib listened and didn't respond. 'I'm 19 and you are already 17,' I added. 'I think it's time.' Grib, who wouldn't move an inch without his brother Barkuna, went and told him where the gold was hidden. Barkuna was married to Sarah by this time and had already fathered one daughter. He was living in Moshe's house and acted like he owned the place. He immediately told his wife about the gold. Unlike naive Grib, who trusted his brother blindly, Barkuna believed that as the oldest and a father, he was entitled to the money: that he should be the heir, not me, Moshe's daughter-in-law.

He and his wife staged a commotion to get everyone out of the house. Then Sarah went to the hiding spots that Grib had shared with them and removed the gold. When Grib later asked his brother what he intended to do with it, Barkuna feigned innocence: 'What gold are you talking about?' he asked. 'The gold Hisne told me about,' Grib answered.

'Let's take a look,' replied Barkuna. 'We'll see if there's really anything there.' They searched the hding places, but of course nothing was left. Barkuna suggested calling me in. 'Perhaps we're not looking in the right places, or maybe Hisne just made up the entire story.'

Grib called me over to point out the places where the gold was hidden. I immediately realized what a foolish thing he had done, but walked over just to confirm that there was nothing there.
'See?' exclaimed Barkuna. 'Empty!'
I shot him a bitter look. Why was Barkuna asking me about gold when he wasn't supposed to know about it in the first place? I gave Grib a disappointed look. 'I told you where the gold was, but not for you to tell your brother!' I yelled at him. 'You're the one who told them, now you deal with it and wait for your brother to spare you some money.'

"Following Barkuna's ugly trick, I hurridly left the room," recalled Hisne. "The two brothers began fighting vehemently, and quickly resorted to yelling and mutual slander. Luckily, all the neighbors around were relatives, so the loud fight stayed within the family.

Grib blamed Barkuna for stealing the money. 'You took the gold,' he told him. 'It's impossible that father never had any money. He was very rich. I told you where the gold was hidden and you stole it!'
'Father was rich, but he wasn't stupid,' replied Barkuna. 'He would never have told Hisne, of all people, where the money was hidden. And you saw for yourself that the hiding spots she mentioned were empty. Father told me where the money is, and now I have it; and for your information, there's not a lot of it. Now let's go inside the house and divide it as fairly as possible.'
Barkuna quickly added, 'Since I'm the oldest, and already have a family of my own, and since this is the way things are done here, I will take two-thirds and you take one-third.'
'A third of what?' screamed Grib. 'Show me the gold!'
Barkuna quickly pulled out a small amount of money he had prepared in advance and stuck it in Grib's hand. 'This is your third,' he told him.
'A third of what?' repeated Grib. 'Show me the rest of it.'
Barkuna refused. 'I'm telling you, this is your third,' he claimed brazenly. 'In fact, there's even a little bit more than a third here. Use this to pay Hisne's bridewealth.'
'What are you talking about?' screamed Grib. 'Father was supposed to pay the bridewealth himself. Now that he's dead and you've inherited his role, you're the one who should pay it. You're the guardian now. You took the house - now be the father.'
The fight went on for hours, getting louder and louder. The two could not agree on how to divide the money, and certainly not on who should pay the bridewealth.

The house wasn't even mentioned - they both took for granted that it belonged to Barkuna. The situation got worse and worse.
Being so poor, and seeing that the gold I was supposed to receive would never reach me, I decided to take a stand. My fiance was not a person I could count on to do this - I knew I could only trust myself, so the next day I approached Grib and Barkuna. There was no way to talk to Grib one-on-one; he was stuck to Barkuna more than ever. They spent all their time together. They held the gold - to be precise, Barkuna held the gold - and they shared it with no one, not even their siblings.
I approached them and told them that I wanted to make true my engagement. I also told my parents about my wish to either marry Grib or have him release me once-and-for-all from my engagement. 'You're not getting out of the engagement,' my father told me firmly. I realized that cancelling the engagement meant that my father would have to pay back the first half of the bridewealth that he had received upon the engagement announcement. Even worse, it meant that he would not receive the second half. That's why he was so against the idea.
When I told Barkuna and Grib about my wish to marry, they responded with hostility. 'We don't want you,' they said. 'You're not the good girl we thought you were.' Their aunt, as well as Barkuna's wife, stepped forward too and began insulting and humiliating me with a whole range of slurs that I won't repeat.
'We don't want you in our family,' they said to me. My brother Shmuel witnessed it too. Shmuel, Sarah and I were all united. Shmuel, a strong and athletic man, could solve any problem with brute force. No one could stand up to him. We always completed each other - he was the force and I was the brains. In fact, he never did anything without consulting me first. But when he the humilliation bestowed by our cousins, he wanted to

strike them as hard as he could. Our neighbors had to hold him down so he wouldn't lose control.

'Is this what you wanted? To be trampled upon for a little bit of money?' he yelled to our parents. 'Where is your dignity? Where is my sister's dignity? I will not let them crush it! They don't want her...? Well we don't want them. Whoever dares speak to my sister, even half a word, will feel my wrath. I will break them apart, all of them.'

After everything cooled down, I went to visit Makdasi, one of the wisest men of the village and the head of the Jewish community. He was known as a problem-solver. I told him my situation and explained to him the three options I faced: one, marry Grib; two, leave for Baghdad; three, convert to Islam.

Makdasi was sitting with his assistant Jacob, who was a distant relative of mine. When Jacob heard my words he told Makdasi that I was right. Makdasi, startled, said to me, 'Don't do it, my child... Don't convert to Islam. We will find a solution for your problem.' He immediately sent Jacob to call in Papirko, the Mukhtar.

Papirko arrived right away and after hearing my story, asked me whether I had anyone by my side.

'Of course,' I replied. 'My mother, my father, my brother and my three sisters.' Papirko said, 'Well then, do this. Tell your parents to sell all their belongings. I will arrange a car to take you to Mosul. There you can get on a train to Baghdad. Go there. In Baghdad you'll find a large Jewish community, rich Jews, you can start a new life there.'

"Mukhtar Papirko was the only one who could grant me the right to leave the village apart from my fiance. But even he couldn't cancel the engagement and let me marry another man.

I returned to my parents and told them about my meeting with Makdasi and the three options we had discussed. I also told them about the Mukhtar's advice. 'You need to sell everything,' I told them, 'because in a

few hours a car will come to take us to Mosul.'
My father had been contemplating leaving Akra even before my announcement. 'We have nothing to sell,' he told my mother. 'We'll take with us what we can carry - clothes and a few kitchen utensils. We'll sell the pots.' Of course we ended up selling nothing, because no one was buying. We packed the little we had and walked to Makdasi's house. He asked his wife to prepare lunch so that we could eat before the car arrived.
The driver in charge of bringing the mail from Akra to Mosul arrived after two hours. Having enjoyed our last meal in Akra, we got in the car and left without saying goodbye to any of our cousins or other family members, not even my fiance.
My situation was complex. On the one hand, I was engaged, and no one could ask for my hand in marriage. On the other hand, my fiance was left behind in Akra, and who knew whether we would ever meet again. I was tied to a man who was one of the reasons why I was leaving town. I knew that I could be free only if he found me and produced a document with his own signature, saying he was letting me go. The only other option was for me to convert my religion.
We arrived in Mosul, penniless. There was no one to greet us, nowhere for us to live, not even enough money for train tickets. We got out at the city center, keeping in mind our destiny: Baghdad. We didn't ask about the Jewish neighborhood; we didn't want anyone's help. We just wanted to arrive at Baghdad and leave our past behind.
We finally arrived at the train station, without any money for tickets. We found a small room inside the station and decided to settle there. There were a few more homeless people there, each lurking in their own corner. The place was large and we didn't mind the company.
The only way to get money for the train ride was to do

porterage work. My father and Shamca, who was 18, went to the market to work for a few days until they could earn enough money for the ride. Whenever they returned from the market, they would bring back a bit of bread, watermelon, or melon. That was all the food we had. Another thing I remember from Mosul are the lice that were everywhere. Anywhere you sat, everywhere you turned, they were there; everyone was scratching. Finally, after seven days in Mosul, we boarded the train to Baghdad. We bought only five tickets - we hid little Mame and Ruhama under the train benches. I don't really remember the train ride because I slept the whole way through. How could I not? All the trauma I had gone endured that past month had worn me down and taken all my strength.

We arrived at Baghdad before dawn. We rode the train all night. Once again, no one came to greet us upon arrival. We asked around to find the Jewish neighborhood.

We were directed toward a place called Khan Najab. It was a neighborhood made of courtyards; each court had 15-20 families. In the center of each court was a well, around which were doors to the apartments. Each apartment was a single room that housed an entire family - sometimes even an extended family.
Realtors would walk around between the courts and connect apartment seekers with homeowners. Each realtor had a region. The realtor in charge came to us to ask what we were looking for. 'We're a seven-member family and we want to live here, near the Jewish community,' my father told him.
'I have a room for you,' he announced happily. 'Even if you have no money - which is usually the case with people who escape from Kurdistan - you can come in and live here. You will work in other Jewish homes doing housework like cleaning, cooking and laundry. With the money you receive, you can pay the rent and my realtor fees.'
The realtors also knew where to find work, mostly housework, in the homes of rich people. When the realtor helped someone find a job, he took the first paycheck as his fee. It covered the room fee as well.
To our great surprise, in the first courtyard we entered we met Elo, who had run away with us from Barzan and made his way with us to Akra. He left Akra two years before us. Elo, who was a widower with two children, stopped in Mosul on his way to Baghdad, met a Jewish widow and mother of two named Hayate, and married her. In Baghdad, they had two children together, so his family now included six children - a big family, in keeping with Kurdish tradition.

Elo let us into his home. His wife gave us cold water, fruit and dates. We quickly learned that dates were Iraq's official fruit. Iraqis cooked dates, baked dates, made honey from honey, and more. Dates grew in every corner. What the nut and the acorn are for Kurdistan, the date is for Iraq.

'You've arrived just in time,' Elo told us. 'You have no idea what things were like here a year ago...' He lowered his voice to a whisper and said, 'We had horrific pogroms. The Muslims killed Jews left and right.'

I was shocked. 'What are you talking about?' I asked him. 'We've been running from them all our lives! They bothered us in Kurdistan, too. My grandfather Haim and his brother Isaac were murdered by Muslims not far from Barzan. Their bodies were thrown in the river and found a few days later - surely you remember that even better than I do!'

'No, no, you don't understand,' murmered Elo. 'Hundreds of Jews have been killed here. Pogroms went on for two or three days and no one said a word, not the government and not even the British.'

Elo was referring to the Farhud, the horrible pogrom unleashed upon the Jews of Baghdad during the Shavuot holiday of 1941. We knew Elo to be calm, modest and quiet. We'd never seen him so agitated. He always told us such wonderful stories. This time he was so upset, he was shaking and sweat appeared on his brow. 'Horrible... horrible...a horrible thing happened here.'

Even in Kurdistan, we had felt the change coming over the Muslims in their attitude towards the Jews. The incidents were minor, but they did point to a larger ongoing trend. When we arrived at Harran, the Muslims there also bothered us. They would hide and wait for us on the roads or by the spring. For our family, the peak incident was the theft of the wool. Things had gotten so bad we had to escape Harran. But they were not any better in Akra - we worked hard but our neighbors never

stopped harassing us, just because we were Jewish.
These were certainly not the same Muslims who had celebrated the Jewish holidays with us: not the same Muslims who picked fruits and vegetables for us on the Sabbath and placed them on our doorstep to help us keep the Sabbath.

A few more words about that time and the changes that took place in Kurdistan, Iraq, and the entire Middle East. In Kurdistan, Jews felt the change in Muslim attitude only somewhat. I'm referring mostly to the years from 1932 to 1942. The Kurdish revolt, which began in 1927, grew stronger over time. It forced the Jews into a situation of perpetual escape. Muslims took advantage of the mess in order to vent their anger on the Jews. This went on for five years, after which the Jewish situation only grew worse and worse.

In 1932, the British Mandate over Iraq ended and the country received its independence. One year later King Faisal died. His son Ghazi was made king in his stead. Since then, and up to 1942, Iraq saw a era of government instability which originated with the fighting between the fascist nationalists who supported Germany, Italy and Spain in the war, and those who were pro-British.

Between 1932 and 1941, the head of the German Embassy in Baghdad was the Middle East scholar, Dr. Fritz Grobba. The embassy, which he led, worked to establish a relationship with the elite, and supported fascist and anti-semitic activity. Intellectuals and military leaders were invited to visit Germany as guests of the Nazi party. Besides influencing various government officials, Nazi Germany's attempts to affect the region were manifested by inserting anti-semitic propaganda into newspapers. The German embassy purchased the paper Al Alam Al Arabi ("The Arab World"). Here, they published propaganda pieces as well as chapters of Adolf Hitler's Mein Kampf translated to Arabic, beginning in October of 1933.

The anti-semitic propaganda was lead by a fascist group headed by Iraqi officials. In 1939, Jerusalem's Mufti Haj Amin al-Husseini arrived in Baghdad. He soon became part of the incitement against the Jews in Iraq. Syrian expatriates were also taking part in these groups. Overt incitement against the Jews was everywhere - in public demonstrations, in posters and in newspapers.
In addition to the fascist groups, Iraq established the youth movement, Al Fatwa, named after an order of the Muslim knighthood. The movement acted just like the Hitlerjugend groups in Germany. In 1938, a representative on its behalf took part in a Nazi convention in Nuremberg. The head of the Hitlerjugend, Baldur von Schirach, even visited Baghdad at one point. Beginning in 1939, all high-school students and teachers were forced to join Al Fatwa, which boasted 63,000 members.
On April 1, 1941, the rebellion of Rashid Ali al-Gaylani began in Iraq. During the revolt, the administration was taken over by a group of pro-Nazi military officers led by Rashid Ali. Throughout the war, harassment of Jews increased, especially outside of Baghdad. On

May 31st, an armistice was signed between the Iraqi government and the British, though the British armed forces remained on the outskirts of Baghdad. Pogroms were carried out during the two days between the signing of the armistice and the British army entering the city on June 2nd.

When the Rashid Ali rebellion broke out, the propaganda against the Jews worsened. Author Sami Michael, who witnessed the pogroms, said the incitement against Jews was all over the local radio and on Arabic Radio Berlin. Of the atmosphere in the street he said: 'On the way to the school, I saw slogans written on the walls announcing that Hitler was eliminating the bacteria... on Muslim shops they wrote the word مسلم, which is Arabic for Muslim, so if a pogram was carried out, the store would not be harmed.

After the British Mandate ended, Iraq took steps to tie the hands of Jews who had political influence and enjoyed financial prosperity. In 1934, dozens of Jewish government officials were fired from the Ministry of Economy and the Ministry of Transportation. In 1935, they unofficially began to limit the number of Jewish students in state-funded schools. In 1936, 300 Jewish government officials were fired, many with high-ranking positions. In 1938, the newspaper Al Hazad, owned by Jews, was shut down. In 1939, restrictions were imposed on Jewish education, and all Jewish education was reduced.

When the Arab revolt in Palestine began, there was a major escalation in anti-Jewish harassment in Iraq. On the eve of the Jewish New Year - September 16, 1936, three Jews were murdered. On Yom Kippur, a bomb was thrown into a temple in Baghdad, with no injuries. During the Rashid Ali rebellion, demonstrations took place in big cities and often ended with Jews being injured.

Members of Al Fatwa were organized into armed

groups called Kataib Al-Shabaab, meaning: youth brigade. They received policing powers, which were used for persecuting Jews. Jews were arrested and tortured on espionage charges, alleging they helped pass information to British airplanes. A lot of money was taken from the Jewish community for fighting the British. Many assets were confiscated, including two Jewish school buildings.

On May 16, 1941 the British Army conquered Basra, though they prefered to position their forces outside the city. On the 19th of May, Jewish shops in town were vandalized and looted.

The Farhud began in the morning of June 1, 1941. It started in the Baghdad neighborhood Al-Karkh, near the Al-Khir bridge. A group of Jewish dignitaries were attacked as they returned from a festive reception in the Palace of Flowers in honor of Abd al-Ilah, the crown prince. This is same area where Saddam Hussein's As-Salam palace was later built.

During the pogrom, 179 Jews were slaughtered and buried in a mass grave. 2,118 Jews were injured and 242 children were orphaned. In addition, property was stolen from approximately 50,000 people.
Shalom Darwish, who was one of the leaders of the Jewish community in Baghdad later recalled that a few days before the massacre, Jewish homes were marked with a handprint - a hamsa - painted red by the members of Al Fatwa.
Two days before it began, Rabbi Sasson Kaduri, head of the Jewish community, was summoned to a meeting with Yunis al-Sabawi, a minister in Rashid Ali's government who declared himself the governor of Baghdad. Al-Sabawi recommended that Kaduri tell his congregation to store up some food, and stay at home for three days in order to protect themselves, since if they went out to the street they could be attacked. It was later established by a governmental investigation that Al-Sabawi intended to annihilate the Jews. His reign only lasted a few hours, and his position was soon taken over by a committee for public safety.
In the afternoon, riots broke out on Ghazi street - which today is known as Kifah Street - in Bab al Sheikh, a Muslim neighborhood. They quickly spread to the old Jewish quarter, and to Jewish neighborhoods in Al-Rusafa. The rioters split into groups and divided the roles between themselves. Any attempt by the Jews to bribe cops into protecting them failed. The pogrom worsened on the second day, kindled by inflammatory

speeches made in the mosques.

During the riots, shops were looted and burned, Temples were vandalized and Torah books were destroyed. The rioters murdered and raped. They killed and tore babies, women and old people to pieces. Joseph Nimrodi, who witnessed the pogrom, said of the event: 'Beyond the window we could see dozens of people armed with knives, axes and guns. Some were carrying furniture and other objects they had stolen from Jewish homes. I saw a woman carrying a baby's foot for its hajal (a golden foot bracelet).'

All the while the British forces were stationed outside of town, on the banks of the Tigris (Hiddekel) River. The Commander of the Armed Forces, Sir Kinahan Cornwallis, refused to let his chief officers into the city to stop the massacre, even though they urged him to do so. British forces only entered the city after the riots were halted by Iraqi forces which were loyal to the crown prince. On the afternoon of June 2, the British imposed a curfew over the city and shot any rioters that remained.

There were also examples of sheer bravery, as members of other religious groups risked their lives in order to save their Jewish neighbors.

Hisne shared more details of those first few days in Baghdad, "After Elo scared us to death, and having realized we have to keep a low profile, we went out to the courtyard. The realtor was waiting for us there. He pointed to one of the doors. It was a fairly large room with nothing inside it. Sometimes, if you got lucky, you might find a bed or a closet in the room. This one was completely empty."

The yards in Khan Najab were large and square, and in the center of each was a water well. Around it were openings to the rooms. Most of the residents in these yards were Jewish Kurds who fled the war and came to the big city to find work, make a living, and escape the hunger and disease. Every yard had Jews from different villages, so a variety of languages was spoken. They all spoke Kurdish, but in many different dialects.
After a few days in Khan Najab, we managed - thanks to our realtor - to find work in cleaning, cooking and even in local factories. I found employment with a fabric factory, while my sister Sarah did cleaning work in a hospital. Shamca was sent to work in the home of one of the richest men in Baghdad, Khuduri Asmieh. It was a huge house with many servants. Shamca didn't have to return home after a day's work, since they set up a bed for him in the room where the house chef lived, a Jew named Ezra.
We had to adapt to a new language. In Akra, Iraqi Arabic was hardly spoken - it was used mostly by Muslims, along with Kurmanji, which was their mother tongue. We had little connection to them so we rarely spoke Arabic. But in Baghdad, Iraqi Arabic was the state language. If we needed to make arrangements with any state institution - the army, police, government offices, or even simply converse in the street - we had to use Iraqi Arabic.
After a meal, Shamca was once asked by his masters

to bring them 'masach thum', literally translated to mouth cleaner. He brought back a towel. The mistress smiled and dragged this tall young man by his ear to the fridge. She opened the door, pointed to the fruit and said, 'See? That's a masach thum. We Iraqis like to clean our mouths with a dessert of fruit, not a towel...'

That's just one example of the kind of things we had to deal with. A new language, a new culture, a new world. But it was worth it - this was much better than anything we ever had before.

One of the things we learned in Baghdad was how to keep quiet. If you wanted to survive, you had to act as if you didn't exist. Khuduri Asmieh had four sons and two daughters. They were a very well-known, highly respected family in Baghdad. His oldest daughter was married to Dr. Gorji Rabieh, who was a very important doctor in Baghdad. One day, while working in his clinic, two masked men came in, covered his head with a piece of cloth and kidnapped Dr. Rabieh. He told everyone the story during one of the meals in Khuduri Asmieh's house.

Shamca, who was serving the meal, managed to understand the story despite his loose grasp of the language. The doctor told how the men grabbed him and drove him around, his eyes covered, for some 15-20 minutes. Perhaps the distance was even shorter and they toured the neighborhood to confuse him. Either way, after about 20 minutes of driving, they brought him down the stairs into some sort of warehouse or shelter, where they removed his blindfold. They sat him on a chair, across from a scared girl who was sitting on a couch.

'We want you to check whether this girl is pregnant,' they ordered the doctor.

'I realized she wasn't married and must have dishonored her family,' told Dr. Rabieh. 'A quick examination proved that she was indeed pregnant. I told them so. They asked

to pay me for my work. Shaking with fear, I told them I wanted no payment - only to be returned home. They covered my eyes and 20 minutes later we arrived at my clinic. They instructed me to keep the blindfold on for five more minutes. I waited as I was told, and only then removed it.'

The doctor, who had so far kept this story a secret, didn't hesitate to share it now, completely ignoring Shamca's presence in the room. Iraqi Jews treated our presence like air - as if we didn't exist at all - as if we came from another planet and didn't understand their culture. Even so, they helped us out a lot, especially in dealing with the state authorities.

During the next few months, we were visited time and again by Jews and Muslims who came to ask for my hand in marriage. Being engaged - even though my husband-to-be was still in Akra - I couldn't accept any of the offers, not that I wanted to. My father wanted very much for me to marry. Our financial situation was not good, and a wedding (and especially the wedding gifts) would really help. But as hard as things got, my parents never once considered handing me over to a Muslim.

When our hardships worsened, my father asked me what I thought we should do. I was almost 20 and knew that we had to come up with a solution soon: either my fiance would come and marry me here, or I needed to somehow break off the engagement.

'No problem,' I told my father. 'Go to the post office. They have people there who can write any letter you dictate to them. Ask them to send it to Grib in Akra. Ask him to send us a signed document from the Ministry of Internal Affairs in Erbil, releasing me from my engagement and allowing me to marry someone else here in Baghdad.'

My father gave me a stern look. 'That means we will have to pay him back the wedding gifts he paid us for the engagement. Where exactly are we supposed to find the money?' he asked. 'First send the letter,' I told him.

'Let's see how he reacts.' My father wasn't convinced. 'Just know that either way, if we have to pay him back - it's on you,' my father replied.
'No problem,' I answered. 'Just send the letter.'
My father went to the post office and mailed the letter to Grib. A few weeks passed and we heard nothing from him. Suddenly, one evening, Grib showed up with his brother Gado, carrying a big bag of his belongings - everything he owned. He brought pans, plates, clothes and more. He placed the bag in the center of the room. In one hand he was also carrying a leather pouch tied with a string, the kind of pouch they used for keeping gold lira. He walked up to my father and said: 'I want to marry Hisne. Here's your money.'
My father took the money and asked Grib if he was planning on taking me back to Akra.
'No,' replied Grib. 'I'm staying here.' Shamca, who was also present, suddenly leapt to his feet, grabbed the money, threw it at Grib's feet and started screaming.
'Take your money! We are just fine without you. We don't need you or it. You love your money - mit parre wetun - your entire life all you were thinking about was money. Not our family, not my sister's honor, only money, money, money. Go back to where you came from before I unleash my anger at you and your brother!'
Hearing the fight, all the residents of the courtyard stepped outside. 'But I want to get married,' Grib told Shmuel, with Gado standing beside him and nodding in approval. My father, too, showed his approval of this marriage. Shmuel, who was being held in place by some of the neighbors, stepped onto a pile of blankets that was lying in the yard and started yelling at our father. 'This is all you want - money. Even you care only about the money. After all the humiliations we endured in Akra, after all he and his brother and his wife and his aunt did to us, you're willing to grovel to them for a few golden coins? No way. Not while I have a say in the matter!' He

ran towards Grib. The neighbors held him again and tried to calm him down.

Then old man Sabto showed up. He was a solemn and respected man. He had a long, white beard and his eyes were a deep blue. His soft and confident voice worked like magic on Shamca. He held Shamca's hands and ordered him to sit down.

'I want to tell you something,' started old man Sabto, so named because of his age and appearance. His voice was so quiet and peaceful that he could barely be heard. 'Haram, - it is forbidden. The boy put his pride aside and came all the way from Akra. He is an orphan, he has nowhere else to be.' Shamca listened and cooled down. 'Today, you are the one agreeing to protect him,' explained Sabto, helping ease my brother's mind. 'You're one step above him, meaning: the tables have turned. Accept him. After all, he's your cousin. Who do you want your sister to marry, one of Baghdad's Muslims? Or perhaps a Jew from Zakho, Amadiya or Dohuk, someone you don't even know? He's your cousin. He's an orphan and he needs your patronage.'

Shmuel had calmed down. He looked at me, waiting to see my response. I nodded. After a long silence he replied, 'Fine. But in addition to her bridewealth, he has to bring her whatever she asks for.'

Sabto agreed. 'What would you like, daughter? Do you agree to marry him? If so, ask for whatever your heart desires.'

"I pondered silently for a long while. 'A golden necklace,' I finally declared. 'In addition to the bridewealth he is paying my father. He can use the many gold lira he and his brother Barkuna own. I know they have a lot... Before he died, his father told me where the money was hidden. I want him to make me a necklace from melted lira - that's all I want.'

Sabto looked at Shmuel and then at me, completely ignoring my parents. At that moment he understood who made all the real decisions in our family. Like in the old days, during our childhood, I was once again the brains and he was the force.

'So are we in agreement?' Sabto asked Grib. 'We're in agreement,' everyone answered, and all the yard's residents began singing.

I was embarrassed. I glanced at my parents. They were smiling, but they also looked a little uneasy. They were happy that their wish had come true and they were to receive their wedding gifts. But it was not complete joy. It was tainted by insult for being left out of the decision making. They realized their hegemony was taken from them and passed on to Shamca and myself. In fact - modesty aside - it was mostly passed to me, since Shamca himself also depended on me.
Once the details were settled, Gado returned to Akra to inform the family about the upcoming wedding. Grib stayed with us, and two weeks later we got married. None of Grib's relatives showed up to celebrate. Not Gado, not his wife and children, not Abd al-Rahman, not even Barkuna and his wife Sarah. Grib was all alone and orphaned.

The wedding was held in our courtyard. My mother and my sister Sarah, along with the other women of the yard, cooked "salona" - fish stews. The wedding was extravagant and luxurious. Sixteen trays held the very best fruits and treats of Iraq. The women of the yard baked mountains of Kurdish breads: lakhma smoka, kadeh, nask naan and more. The davul-zurna players warmed our hearts with music.
The whole event was three days of food, dancing and singing, involving all the Jews from the area yards. Over 100 people danced in circles in the courtyard. Old man Sabto's family and Jews from Dohuk and Sandur that lived in the area filled in for Barkuna's family members, who never showed.
Several weeks after the wedding, Gado arrived at Baghdad with his entire family, escorted by Abd al Rahman. Gado, Chizeme and their three children moved to Baghdad permanently. They rented a room in a yard near ours. Barkuna remained with his family in Akra, in the house he inherited from his father. Abd al Rahman

also went back to Akra, to be with the woman he loved. Now that we were married, Grib and I moved to a nearby khan, and rented our own room. Grib, who was hardworking and energetic, quickly found a housekeeping job. My father, who was the legal guardian of me and my brother, became Grib's guardian too. As such, he was the one to receive our paychecks every weekend - back then, it was customary to pay the head of the family, not the worker.

Every Friday, when we were supposed to receive our pay, my father went over and collected everyone's pay: mine, my husband's and my siblings'. 'You live with me and eat my food, therefore I hold the money,' my father used to say. He took the pay and distributed the money as he saw fit. Grib, naively and because he didn't have much of a choice, agreed to it without a word.

I once bravely took some money from my husband. I bought some pink velvet fabric, gave it to a seamstress in the fabric factory in which I worked, and asked her to make me a jacket. I was suffering from the cold and needed something warm to wear. My father saw me in my jacket and slammed my head against the wall. 'We're starving and you go out and buy yourself clothes?' he screamed angrily and hit me again and again.

Even though I was married and did not belong to my father anymore, I suffered the insult and the pain. My face swelled up until I could hardly see. My head was in a lot of pain. My husband saw my face and asked what had happened. When I told him the story, he kept silent and did nothing. After a few minutes he mumbled, 'That's what your father is like...'

The next morning I went to work. When my manager saw my face, she was horrified. 'I fell and hurt myself,' I lied.

'Come on,' she said. 'I'll make you something to drink.' She looked at me with suspician, not believing the story I had made up. 'I'll pour you a glass of tea,' she offered

again. I refused and thanked her for worrying for me. I told her a glass of water would suffice and that I'd pour it myself.

In those days, we were all very wary of Muslims. We didn't even trust those who worked with us. We knew they might put something in our drinks, because it had happened before. I poured myself a glass of water and went to my work station in the factory.

'Sit here,' my line manager said. 'You shouldn't work today. Rest and take care of your wounds and we'll pay you your salary.'

A few weeks passed in the same way, with my father picking up our paychecks every Friday. One day I decided to put an end to it. 'You're right about Shmuel and Sarah,' I told him, 'but you can't take pay for me and Grib anymore. I'm married and I don't live under your roof anymore. This can't go on like this. Grib and I will pick up our own pay, starting this Friday.' Surprisingly, that's exactly what we did.

We really felt like things were finally working out and we had found our peace. We were all working, making our living, 'every man under his vine and under his fig tree'.

But it couldn't last. Like a thunderstorm on a summer's day, new trouble came to our doorstep. Well, we couldn't expect to be the only people in the world whose lives ran smoothly...
A few months after the wedding, my parents were visited by representatives of the Iraqi Army, trying to recruit Grib and Shmuel. We were astounded. How did they even find us? We only recently arrived from Kurdistan. While it's true that we'd come from Iraqi Kurdistan, I didn't recall us listing ourselves with any institution, apart from registering our engagement and subsequent marriage. It was a real mystery.
The more I thought about it the more I decided that my brother and my husband must have registered somewhere in Akra. Once they reached enlisting age, the army must have sent someone to pick them up from our old home in Akra - but could only find Barkuna. He probably paid his own way out of enlisting and gave them our address in the Khan Najab, and that's how they knew to find us.
By then, I was already in an advanced stage of pregnancy, but that wasn't enough to excuse my husband from military service. We had to pay to get his exemption. It cost us 50 dinars, a substantial sum for a couple in our situation. Shmuel, on the other hand, enlisted in the army. It was customary in Iraq for men to pay 50 dinars if they refused to enlisted, but my parents didn't have that kind of money, nor did I or my sister Sarah. Sarah was working in households for very rich people, so she asked them what she should do about Shamca.
'We will pay for it,' they told her. 'You can pay us back in payments when you find the money.' What they

wanted in exchange, was for us to give them a deposit - a valuable object worth at least 50 dinars.

When Sarah told me this, I answered 'no problem' and took off the golden necklace I had received from Grib. 'Here, give them this,' I said, handing her the necklace. 'We will work, the two of us, and pay back the money for Shmuel's dismissal.'

Sarah took the necklace and hurried to the home of her employers. 'Here, this necklace is worth far more than 50 dinars. Take it and give me the money.' The employer saw the necklace and replied, 'Don't worry, we will take care of everything.'

'What do you mean?' asked Sarah. 'We will go to the army offices,' he answered. 'We will see what can be done and do everything we can to release your brother.' Sarah returned to me and told me about the conversation. 'And do you trust them?' I asked. 'Why do you ask?' wondered Sarah. 'Do they look suspicious to you?'

'I don't know,' I answered. 'I suspect they might be able to release Shmuel without paying anything at all, being Iraqi citizens. They will take our 50 dinars and keep it.' After further consideration, I decided it didn't really make a difference. We would have to part with the money one way or another, whether we paid it ourselves or got someone else to pull some strings.

In the meantime, my brother was recruited into the Iraqi Army. He was stationed in Mosul, where he completed basic training. During training, he visited Akra, where he could have visited Barkuna and Sarah. Suspecting they were the ones who informed the army of his whereabouts, he never bothered to go see them, though he did visit some other friends and neighbors.

After a while the exemption payment reached the army. The most they could do at that point was to station him in Baghdad for the next three months, until he was finally released. If it weren't for those 50 dinars, he

would have had to serve for two years. Thanks to the money, it was only for six months.

That 50 dinars took a long time to pay back. We worked hard, each of us in two different jobs every day, until we repaid every last cent and my necklace was returned.

Shamca's life in Kurdistan, which was full of suffering, hunger and hard work, built his strength in body and spirit. As a youth, he was physically big and strong; as an adult, he was a large man with muscular legs and mighty arms.

Walking the long distances with a heavy load on his back while remaining alert and ready for possible dangers like wild animals, kidnapping attempts and harassment, also led to the development of acute instincts.

In Baghdad, life was much more comfortable, particularly after he discovered the chaikhans. These were entertainment venues aimed for men, much like the cafes in the Iraqi market in Mahane Yehuda, Jerusalem or in the Tikva neighborhood of Tel Aviv. The men spent hours there, drinking spicy tea and steamy coffee, playing backgammon, dominoes, and card games.

The name chaikhan comes from the combination of chai, tea, and khan, meaning: a parking spot or way station. Shamca began frequenting these tea houses and spending most of his time there; he learned to play dominoes, a game which he particularly liked and could play for hours.

Most of the chaikhan visitors were Muslim. Some Jews hung around - those who had the courage to socialize with the Arab hegemony - but Jews were really a very small minority in those places.

Occasionally, a fight would break out. Shamca, who was very strong, quickly became the chaikhan king. If a fight broke when he wasn't around, they would come get him from home.

He wasn't particularly eager to fight, but if a Jew was injured he would soon intervene, particularly if the Jew involved was of his own. He never feared taking chances, even though he knew that in Arab culture it

was customary to revenge injuries. When Arabs feel their honor has been besmirched, they take vengeance. Sometimes vengeance came from others, without them even knowing about it. Arabs took revenge every time they felt their personal or national pride had been hurt. The Arabs also respected Shamca. They loved him more than they feared him. Despite his strength and size he was a very friendly and pleasant man who prefered solving problems in peaceful ways. Once in a while, he would invite Muslims to drink tea with him, an act that greatly upset other Jews in the area. When a fight broke out that did not concern him, he would just sit it out, sipping tea and watching with enjoyment.

"In the yard where my parents lived, there were Kurds of all kinds and origins," explained Hisne. "In the room next door lived old Sabto, the respected man who calmed my brother when Grib asked to marry me. He had four children. He came from Zakho, where he was one of the most important men in town. At the time, Zakho was the spiritual center for the entire Iraqi Kurdistan Jewry."

From the 16th century and up to the early 18th century, that spiritual center was Barzan - initially led by Rabbi Samuel Barzani, and later by his daughter Asenath. Barzan's glory as Jewry's spiritual center diminished following the rebellion and wars - primarily due to the many bombings it had endured. In its stead, Zakho - and to some degree Amadiya - became prominent.

Zakho is located in northern Iraq, in the Khabur River Valley, only eight kilometers from the Turkish border and 30 kilometers from the Syrian border. The town was divided into three regions: the Muslim Quarter, which was the largest; and the Christian and Jewish Quarters. Two streams of the Khabur River cross the town. They split in the north-eastern part of town and meet again in the south, becoming one wide river. Where the river splits is a small island - the Jewish Quarter. It was connected to the rest of town with three bridges. The most famous of them, the southern bridge, was also the largest. In Kurdish it was called Gshra Ruwa.

The river was between five and ten meters wide. The water was clean and fresh and used for drinking, cooking and laundry. The river was also used to transport wood from place to place on rafts. In addition, the river bank served as a promenade where children met to play games, and many special occasions were celebrated. Every Thursday, the womenfolk met there to do their laundry, talk and share gossip, and it became a day of recreation. At the end of the day, they filled their vases with water in preparation for the Sabbath.

During the rainy season and when the snows melted, the river would rise and overflow, flooding nearby houses. One of the popular legends in Zakho told of an event that occurred 450 years prior, when the river flooded the entire town. All the residents fled to nearby cities and the town was abandoned. Eventually a forest grew there. Years later, the area's ruling Muslim family - Shamadin, decided to rebuild the city. But every house they built collapsed when finished. They built - and the houses would collapse. They sought advice from the wise men of the region. The wise men said that the town used to house Jews, and it could never be rebuilt unless they convinced the Jews to return. So the Shamadin family went to the Jews who lived by the Turkish border to try and convince them to return - but with no luck, as the Jews were afraid of the river.

One day they found a tall and large Jew who was not afraid. He let everyone know of his decision to return to town. He went to the forest, cut down trees, created a clearing and built his home. Lo and behold - the house did not collapse. He kept cutting down trees, creating more clearings, and building more houses, all of which stood tall and strong. He continued working until the entire forest was replaced by houses.

The Muslims called him The Forest Man, or Dachlika in Kurdish. His descendents lived there until 1950, when the entire Zakho community moved to Israel. According to the stories, there was always a thick tree trunk in Shmuel Dachlika's yard, in memory of the head of the family.

Zakho had two temples. The bigger one was called Cnishta Rabsa, meaning: the large temple, whose hall and yard could host some 2,000 people. The smaller temple could host up to 1,000.

"Back to the yard," Hisne continued. "Our closest neighbor was Sabto. In Zakho he was married to Simha,

and they had a boy - Shabtai. Next to his room were Esther Noah and her two sons, Haio and Noah. Esther was widowed after the two children were born. In order to prevent the children from being adopted by Muslims, Sabto married Esther, in addition to his own wife. He adopted her two children. Some said he married her for the money her late husband left her. About a year after the wedding, they had twins, a boy and a girl. The boy died during labor but the girl survived, and her name was Dina."

Hisne paused. She took a long sip of water and sighed deeply. "Dina was my best friend," she said. "Dina, and my sister Sarah and I were always together. Dina was your mother." Whenever Hisne mentioned my mother, I was very touched. She spoke of her with such warmth. "She was so naive, so modest and honest - no other woman in the world was like her," she said and blew her nose. I was trying hard not to cry.

"About six months after Dina was born, Sabto had another daughter by his wife Simha. She was named Miriam. The two daughters were raised together, and the wives took care of all the children. There was very open hostility between Sabto's two wives. The fights were never-ending and more than once he had to intervene and bring peace - sometimes resorting to physical pressure.

After five years of marriage, Esther passed away. The question was again raised of whether to give the children up for adoption. This time there were three of them: Haio, Noah and Dina - and there wasn't a simple answer. The older boys could find a solution, but Dina, who was much younger, was given away for a short while to a Muslim family, while still maintaining strict Judaism. She stayed with the Muslim family for one year, until she was a little bit older.

Sabto Zaken and his family left Zakho to Baghdad when Dina was 15-years-old. Their move was in response to the many decrees which Iraqis issued for the Kurdistan Jews under the influence of Nazi Germany. This happened while Rashid Ali rose to prominence - he was a fascist and an enemy of the Jews.

It happened in 1941, the year of the Farhud. Rashid Ali ordered the Jews to collect all the gold that was available in town, in order to take it from them. The order was never carried out, because right before it was scheduled to occur, Rashid Ali was taken down by the British. This did nothing to change Sabto's mind. He had already decided to move to Baghdad and to take his daughter Dina with him.

Shortly before their move, his daughter-in-law passed away - that is, the wife of his oldest son Shabtai. The couple had a young son named Shmuel. After his wife died, Shabtai married another woman, but she did not want to take care of Shmuel. Sabto did not want to give the boy up for adoption and decided to raise him with his wife Simha. In fact, the boy's primary caregiver was Dina. Shmuel was a beautiful child with big, blue eyes, fair hair and a particularly good temperament.

One year after their arrival to Baghdad, their daughter Miriam turned 16. Sabto decided to marry her off to Elyahu Ela, whose family was also among former Zakho residents, and among the most important families in town. Sabto sent Dina to Muhammad Aref al-Jazrawi, a Muslim who was one of the greatest Kurdish singers of all time, in order to ask that he sing at her sister Miriam's wedding. Like all weddings, this one took place in the courtyard. Until the wedding, Sabto and his family lived in a room in a yard nearby; after the wedding, the room was given to the young couple and he and his family moved into our yard in Khan Najab - near my parents, David and Zere."

The year was 1944. Hisne and Grib, who had been married for one year, had their first child. Grib named him Moshe, after his father who had died four years earlier in Akra.

Two years later, in 1946, Hisne had another son; they named him Naji. In those days it was trendy to give children newer Kurdish names rather than biblical names which were more popular in Kurdistan. These names were given to both Arab and Jewish children.
Hisne and Grib fit in well with the Jewish society of Baghdad. They adopted many of the customs, including the choice of their son's name.
Meanwhile, between the birth of Moshe and Naji, another event took place which tied the Baruch-Barkuna family of Barzan to the Zaken family of Zakho. Shamca, Hisne's brother, fell for Dina. He asked his parents to turn to Sabto and ask for her hand - that was how things were done. His mother, Zere, refused.
'We don't want her,' she responded. 'She's not from the same origins as we are, and she's too thin. She hardly has any breasts, and I don't believe she could ever give birth.' Dina was indeed a very thin girl; she was also shy and slightly cross-eyed. 'I heard a rumor in the yard,' added Zere, 'that she doesn't even get her period.'
Shamca heard his mother's words and did not insist. To an outsider, it almost looked like he forgot all about it; but in truth, his love for Dina was burning within him. A few months later he told Hisne his secret. He told her of his love for Dina and of their parents' refusal to ask for her hand on his behalf. He even told her about their mother's comments. Hisne, who was already a mother herself, offered to look into it for him. She let Sarah in on the secret, and together the two sisters tried to find out the truth about Dina.
One day a bris was celebrated for one of the families. Hisne overheard Simha, Sabto's wife, order Dina to

remain outside, stating that she wasn't allowed to come in. Hisne's eyes lit up. She immediately ran to her sister with the news that Dina had started her period. 'I heard it with my own ears! I heard Simha telling her she's not allowed to come in for the bris, and that she must remain outside...' The two sisters told Zere the news.
'It's possible that she has gotten her period,' agreed Zere, 'but she has no breasts. Shamca is my only son and it is important that he has healthy offspring - that's the only way our family heritage can continue.'
'You don't have to have large breasts to have children,' Hisne replied. 'You know that better than I do. When she becomes pregnant her breasts will grow accordingly - you'll see.' Zere listened to her and answered, 'Let me think about it. My son is young, he only just finished his army service. Let time take its toll.'
Shamca couldn't bare the pain of his love any longer. He went to see Hisne again. 'I cannot go on like this,' he confessed. 'Either marry me to Dina or else I'll run away to Basra. I'll throw myself in the river and try for the other side. Whatever happens, happens: if I die, that's fine; if I survive I'll get on the train to Basra.'
'Wait just a little bit longer,' encouraged Hisne, who was pregnant again. 'Let me get through this pregnancy and then I'll take care of everything.' That very night she was rushed to the hospital. Shamca followed her there. 'Birth or no birth, I've made up my mind - I'm running away,' he said. 'Just let me get through with the birth, I'll help you, I promise,' begged Hisne. 'Do what you want, I can't stay here anymore,' replied Shamca in despair. 'You'll find me over the river, maybe in Basra, if I survive...'
After Naji was born, Hisne decided to approach Sabto herself in order to ask for Dina's hand in marriage. In the meantime she sent Grib to look for Shamca and tell him everything was being taken care of - he was to promise him that Dina would be his wife. Hisne went to Sabto's home and politely asked to speak with him. 'Sit down,

daughter,' ordered Sabto. 'Tell me - what is this about?'
'I want to ask for Dina's hand for my brother,' answered Hisne. Sabto looked at her and smiled.

'Where are your parents?' he inquired. 'I'm not supposed to discuss this with you; I should be talking to the groom's parents.'

'Forget my parents,' said Hisne. 'I'm here and I represent the family. My parents are not involved in this - they will accept whatever answer I give them.' Sabto replied gravely, 'I know you and I know you are the leader of the house. I know my daughter will be in good hands. If you promise to protect her, I'll make her a servant, the sole of your shoe.'

'She will never be that,' Hisne replied. 'She will be my sister and my friend, but also my sister-in-law, my brother's wife. That is all I want,' she told Sabto.

'Still,' he answered, 'either talk to your parents about it or I will. Tell them I agree.'

Hisne returned home to find out what Grib has discovered in his search for Shamca. Did he find him, or did Shmuel make true his threat and leave for Basra - a 12-hour train ride south?

Apparently Grib found Shamca in one of the chaikhans across the river.

'Hisne took care of everything; you will marry Dina,' promised Grib.

'Are you sure?' asked Shamca. 'If not, I'll throw myself in the river.'

Grib grew annoyed. 'Stop with the river already!'

Shamca was an excellent swimmer. The odds of him drowning were practically zero. One time he went swimming and reached the bottom of the bridge, where there was a strong current caused by the water hitting the pier. Shamca got caught in the turbulence and nearly drowned. He was being pulled under, and every time he tried to rise up out of the water, he was pulled farther down. When he was nearly out of air, he realized that he shouldn't try to rise up but instead, dive deeper and find a way out of the turbulence. Without any air he managed to float and rise to the surface beyond the turbulence and swim towards the river bank.

'Return with me,' said Grib. 'Hisne is waiting for you. She'll explain everything.' He had a way of making everything work out. The two returned home. 'Let's go see mother and father,' instructed Hisne. 'I'll talk them into the idea.'

Zere was concerned about only one thing: what about offspring? 'All will be fine," they promised her. 'If we see there's a problem, Shamca can always get another wife.' This answer reassured her. The parents, along with Shamca and Hisne, went to Sabto's house to declare their agreement to the match. The engagement ceremony took place in the yard that very week.

Now that Shamca was engaged, he grew calmer. When he finished the work day, he would hurry to the house where Dina worked. He never went in - only waited for her outside, sometimes for a whole hour. When she finally came out, his eyes would shine. 'Why did it take you so long?' he asked. 'We've all finished working already.'

'I guess I work slowly... but thoroughly,' she explained.

And so every day he would finish his work and come to Dina's workplace. One day she finished working before he arrived. She went to see him in the house where he worked and stepped inside. He was surprised to see her there.

'I'll be done soon,' he told her.

'I'll wait for you,' she replied.

When he finished work, she asked him to sit with her on the bench - takhta in Kurdish. She brought a washtub - a tashte - placed it before him, added some water, and using a small tool called a dokla began washing his hair. Shamca was incredibly moved. He was thrilled by her kind act. He never told anyone about it until many

years later, when he would often tell of it to his children, almost crying. 'She washed my hair, do you know what that means?' he would ask, unable to contain his emotions. 'She washed my hair before the wedding. That's when I knew that she loved me too, that she wasn't being forced to marry me against her will.'

The same week that his parents met Sabto, Shamca was invited by Sabto to a Sabbath dinner at his home. Sabto, whose two sons were fully literate, performed every Sabbath ritual perfectly. When they returned home from temple, he and his sons would sit at the table. Shabtai, the eldest son, would say kiddush for the wine and the challah bread. Sabto would burst out singing, while his wife Simha served the food.

That Sabbath, Simha prepared her famous wheat dish. The meal was also crafted as a ceremony. Sabto would receive the first plate, a large kutele kubbeh dumpling surrounding by thick wheat soup. Everyone else waited patiently. Sabto would take the spoon and cut the kubbeh in half. If the kaliya, the fat stored in the kubbeh, spilled into the soup with its yellowish-green color, Sabto would nod his head once, in approval. But if it didn't - indicating that there wasn't enough kaliya in the kubbeh - he would eat without nodding his head... Which of course, never happened.

Shamca was highly impressed by his host. There was something noble and respectable about him, something his own father never had.

Sarah found her place in Baghdad too. She got a job at a Jewish-owned hospital. She worked in the maternity ward, cleaning and running errands. The nurses and staff liked her very much, as she was hardworking and loyal.

One day, a girl named Badri was hospitalized in one of the wards. She was different than all the other women Sarah had met - she wore trousers, heaven forbid...
Sometimes she wore a dress on top of the trousers, but she was still very different from everyone else. She was hospitalized several times, not in the maternity ward but in other wards. Anytime she was in the hospital, she livened up the party, and she sang really well, particularly Turkish and Iraqi folk songs. She also liked Sarah a lot and the two became close friends. Sarah would often treat Badri to drinks and fruit after meal time was over. Once, before being released from the hospital, Badri told Sarah that she was leaving and moving to Erbil.
'Yes, I know where that is,' Sarah replied.
'I guess I won't be seeing you anymore,' said Badri, and handed Sarah a note with her new address. 'If you ever need anything - help with the authorities or anything else, write to me and I'll do my best to help you.' The two kissed goodbye. Sarah kept the note, in case she ever needed help.
When Shamca's wedding date was set, Sarah suddenly remembered Badri. 'Remember that I told you about a woman who was hospitalized with us a few times?' she asked Hisne. 'She sings beautifully, and I'd like to invite her to Shamca's wedding. I want to invite her as a friend, but I also want her to sing. She sings so well, and will really add a lot to the celebration.'
'Go to the post office,' Hisne suggested. 'Ask them to write down what you want to say. They will send it to the address you have for her.

Sarah did as she was advised. 'Hello dear Badri,' she dictated to the post office clerk. 'My brother is getting married and I would love for you to join us for the wedding. That way, we could see each other and you can sing at our event. Yours lovingly, Sarah.' The letter was mailed.

The wedding took place in the yard. Once again, there were trays of salona fish stew, a variety of breads, fruit, treats, and plenty of drinks for all. This time, however, they decided to have the wedding in the Jewish-Iraqi tradition, in order to be more like the Baghdad Jewry.

In addition to Badri's invitation, Sarah also invited an Iraqi-style band called Chalri Baghdad. Chalri is a Turkish word meaning, ensemble. The band included two singers and four musicians. This type of band used to perform at both Jewish and Arab events. For this wedding, they replaced the traditional davul-zurna.

The festivities went on for three days - days full of singing, dancing, and another Iraqi custom - renting cabs and riding - the bride, the groom, and the entire family - all around the city, honking the car horns all over town.

Before and during the wedding, Sarah was looking for Badri - but she never arrived. Sarah was disappointed, and told herself that perhaps Badri never received the letter.

After their wedding, Shamca and Dina lived in David and Zere's house along with three of Shamca's sisters: Sarah, Mame and Ruhama. Only later, after they had the chance to work and save some money, were they able to rent a room in a nearby yard.

A few months after the wedding, they had an unexpected visit from police officers and detectives from the gendarmerie, who came to see Sarah at Meir Elias, the Jewish hospital where she worked. The staff saw the officers and panicked - they knew that whenever the gendarmerie arrived, arrests were made.

'Who is Sarah Baruch?' inquired one of the officers.
'That's me,' replied Sarah.
'You're coming with us. You're under arrest. You're being charged for spying for Israel.'
'There must be some mistake,' insisted Sarah. 'I have nothing to do with Israel, and I can't even read and write. I'm a simple woman, a Kurdish woman from the mountains... I don't know what you're talking about, it must be a mistake.'
'No mistake here,' replied the commander. 'You're coming with us right now.'
One of the officers was holding handcuffs and asked to tie her hands. She pulled a money bill out of her dress and shoved it into the officer's hand, requesting not to be cuffed. He obliged her request, and took the money.
'I need to talk to my mother,' pleaded Sarah. 'We live not far from here. I also need to pick up some things to have with me at the station.'
When they arrived at Sarah's house, no one was home. Everyone had gone to work. The neighbors were surprised to see Sarah being led to arrest.
'Let my mother know that I'm being arrested and taken to the police station in Mosul,' she told one of the onlookers.
'I will,' answered the neighbor.
Sarah was brought to the police station in Baghdad, where the officer signed the arrest warrant. At night, they got on the train to Mosul where she would be held in custody.
When Zere returned home, the neighbors informed her that Sarah had been taken to Mosul. Without hesitation, she went after her. She took a bit of money, some dried fruit and water, and headed to the train station. The little money she took was stuffed between her breasts to make sure it was readily available, mostly for bribing policemen. She only managed to get on a train the next evening.

Sarah traveled all night. She couldn't tell what the officers wanted from her. When they arrived at the police station in Mosul, there was no officer to sign her arrest warrant. They took her to another station, but no officer was available there either. They returned to the first station, and lacking an officer, they pushed her into an arrest room and shut the door behind her.
'I was shoved into a dark cell,' recalled Sarah many years later. 'Inside the cell, I immediately noticed Badri's silhouette. 'Hada kulo minnek, kula minkh...' I told her: It's all because of you. We fell into each other's arms.
"Badri held me tight and said, 'Walaishi alleki, kulo alay, inti barria,' meaning: They have nothing on you, it's all about me; you're innocent. As we sat in the corner of the cell, Badri told me in whispers how she was actually an immigration (aliyah) activist. 'I work with the Israeli aliyah envoys,' she explained. 'The authorities found out, and caught me during one of their surveillance exercises. I took out all the papers I had on me and swallowed them. The letter you sent me was in another pocket, so I didn't get the chance to eat it. When they read it, they assumed we worked together and that those two short lines you sent were some kind of secret code regarding my activity. When I told them you were just a friend who invited me to a wedding, they didn't believe me. They questioned whether I was even a singer. Don't worry, the truth will come out and you will get out of this place as a innocent - I swear to you.' "We spent three months in a cell full of lice. Throughout those months, Badri would place my head on her knees so she could remove the lice from my hair. She hugged and patted me, and tried to get them all, but there were so many lice that I can still hear them walking all over my head... Every once in a while, Badri would be taken in for an interrogation which lasted an hour or two. I could hear her screams in the distance. She would always return stumbling. I would ask what they'd done to her. 'Nothing,'

she would reply, 'just a few flaks' (bamboo stick lashes over the feet)."

Meanwhile, Zere arrived at Mosul. She didn't really know the city, since she had only visited once, and even then, just for a few days. She asked around for directions to the Jewish neighborhood. When she found it, she began looking for mezuzot on the doors. As soon as she spotted one, she knocked on the door. All the Jews in Iraq, even in Mosul, lived in fear of the police. When they opened the door for her, they did so very carefully.

'I'm here looking for my daughter,' she told them. 'I've come from Baghdad. They've arrested my daughter for spying for Israel. I don't know why. We have nothing to do with anyone in Israel.'

'They've arrested Jews here for the same reason,' the Jews of Mosul told Zere. 'We know of this happening around here.' They invited her to come in.

'I've brought some dried fruits,' said Zere. 'I want to give them to my daughter. She won't eat the food they offer her - we only eat kosher...'

'Don't worry,' her hosts replied, trying to calm her down. 'We'll give you kosher food to take to her.'

"It was early in the morning," Sarah continued. "The hosts took my mother in, fed her breakfast, and sent her on her way with fine cheeses to bring to me in my cell - but mostly for bribing officers along the way. The policemen happily accepted the cheese, but wouldn't let my mother in. Needless to say, the cheese they promised to give me arrived only in part - most of it was confiscated.

Of course, my mother took all this into consideration in advance. During those three months, my mother visited Mosul a number of times, always staying with the Jewish family for a night or two before returning to Baghdad. Each time she went to the station, she made it all the way to the front door, but they wouldn't let her in. After three months, I was brought before a judge. I

told him that I couldn't read or write, and although I sent that letter to my friend, it was typed for me in the post office.

'Open it, sir, and read what it says,' I told the judge. 'You can see for yourself that it has nothing to do with my accusations.' He opened the note and read it - and indeed he saw there was nothing in it to incriminate me. He also realized he was seeing a simple woman, uneducated, who couldn't possibly have done all the deeds she was being accused of.

'Let her go,' he ordered the policemen. 'She's innocent.' They immediately followed procedure and signed the necessary forms. They took me outside and told me to manage things by myself. Not for a moment did I imagine it going differently; I knew they would never return me to Baghdad. My mother had said that she would wait for me, and upon my release, I knew exactly where to look for her. I went straight to the Jewish neighborhood where she stayed every time she came to Mosul, and there she was. We hugged, kissed and even cried a little.

'What happened?' cried Zere. 'What did they want from you? What did they do to you all this time? Did they give you anything to eat? Did they beat you?' She was very upset, as was I. The neighbors gathered around us as well.

'Do you remember Badri?' I asked my mother. 'The one I invited to Shamca's wedding?'

'Oh, sure, the one from the hospital,' she answered. 'I knew no good would come of her. Couldn't you tell she wasn't like us? Couldn't you see she was different?'

'It's all over. It's done,' I replied. 'I'm innocent - the judge said so. I'm no part of this. Come on, let's go home.'

We parted from the good Jews who had welcomed my mother in their home, and fed her all this while. They gave us food for the road: bread and dried fruit. At night we boarded the train for Baghdad."

The atmosphere in the streets of Baghdad was tense. Jews could not easily get around. They had to blend in and try not to be noticed, which was not a simple task. For Kurdistan Jews, this was doubly hard. Even if they could hide their appearance, they still had to talk, and as soon as they opened their mouths, the unique accent immediately gave them away. They had to speak as little as possible.

Sarah asked to return to her job at the hospital, but was not accepted back. 'While it's true that you're a good and hardworking employee,' they told her, 'we are not interested in hiring someone who was a spy and was in trouble with the authorities.'
'I wasn't in trouble,' she insisted.
'You were. You somehow came out of it innocent, but we don't know how.' That was the reasoning for their refusal to re-hire her. Jews were afraid to work with people whose names had been tarnished by an accusation of aliyah work or spying. For lack of options, Sarah returned to the yards, looking for realtors. She secured some housework with one of the wealthy Jewish families in the area. Some Jewish families remained rich at the time - but not many.
Sarah found a job working for a childless couple who wanted a housekeeper; she worked there for several months. One day, she brought along her sister Mame, who was 14-years-old. She was sweet and obedient and the couple fell in love with her immediately.
'Bring her every day,' they insisted.
Sarah brought Mame to their house every day. She then managed to find work with a woman named Reyna, who was married to Dr. Alex, a German doctor who owned a hospital in Baghdad. Sarah worked for Reyna as a cook, while Mame stayed with the other couple.
Reyna was an educated Jewish woman from Basra. She married Dr. Alex and worked side by side with him.

While working at Reyna's, Sarah overheard a phone conversation which seemed to be with agents for whom Reyna was coordinating the immigration of Jews to Israel. Sarah, whose survival instinct was always on, pretended not to hear. She once heard Reyna shout over the phone: 'I want four planes a day, not one... I don't know how, but you have to arrange at least four flights a day.' Sarah did her cooking and never asked Reyna about these calls, even though the two of them had developed a real friendship.

Eventually, Sarah became Reyna's personal assistant, in addition to being her cook. She accompanied her to the school where Jews who wanted to go to Israel, waited. While Reyna checked their arrangements, Sarah ran errands and made sure the yard was tidy.

The atmosphere in Baghdad worsened once the UN passed the decision regarding the Palestine-Israel division in 1947. This was less than a year before the State of Israel declared its independence. Iraqi authorities began using oppressive measures against the Jews. Thousands of Jews were arrested or taken into special custody for being Zionists. Many others applied for permits to leave for Israel, but soon laws were passed which froze their bank accounts and forbade Jews from selling their property without a special permit.

The Jewish immigrants who did manage to obtain exit permits were not allowed to take more than 50 kilograms of cargo each. Shortly after, a decree was declared which allowed the confiscation of all property belonging to Iraqi Jews who, by the very fact they left the country, had "given up their nationality". A lot of Jewish property was sold in public auctions.

A year later, the Iraqi government passed laws to limit Jewish movement. Jews were not allowed to enter schools, hospitals, or other public institutions. Their requests for the import and export permits needed to continue their business operations, were refused.

Jewish life in Iraq became so difficult that over 110,000 Jews signed up for immigration.

The Jewish community in Iraq was one of the oldest and greatest Jewish communities in the Arab world. In fact, it was the grandest of all Israelite exiles. In 1948, the Jewish population in Iraq was 135,000. Baghdad alone was home to over 77,000 Jews. About a quarter of the wealthy population was Jewish. The Jewish population was rich and prestigious. Until World War II, Jews held powerful positions in import/export as well as high-level government jobs.

Kurdish Jews, on the other hand, were neither rich nor powerful. All they could do was to keep a low profile.

Shamca and Dina continued living in their parents' old house, along with Sarah, Mame and Ruhama. After the wedding, Shamca changed almost beyond recognition. He was influenced by his cousin Gado, a violent bully who often beat his wife.

Our family as a whole had a horrible problem with violence against women. My own father, Shamca, was hardly delicate with my mother - which was unusual among the Kurds.
In Kurdish culture, the attitude toward woman was much more liberal than in the Muslim world. A woman could sit with the men, discuss home economics, and did not have to cover her face; she had the same rights as her husband. They did not have a "master-servant" relationship, as in the Muslim world.
Sabto Zaken, Dina's father, never once hit his wife. Neither did my uncle Binyamin, nor Elo, nor our grandfather, Baruch. The violence in our family came from Moshe, David, Gado and Shamca. On the very first occasion that Shamca became angry with Dina, he hit her. Dina, who was not used to this behavior, ran to her father's house. Shamca was confused; he wasn't sure how to react. He immediately consulted Gado.
'What do you mean, ran away?' Gado was astounded. 'Mkhila kam pehne,' he said, meaning: Kick her away. 'I'll come with you to Sabto's house,' added Gado, who wanted to make sure Shamca was doing as he was told. 'I'll wait for you outside, but I want to see you kick her out of that house and kick her all the way back to your own house.'
That is exactly what happened.
Shamca entered Sabto's house and without a word began kicking Dina with all his strength. This all happened in the presence of Yehuda, Dina's younger brother, as well as her sister Miriam and her husband Elyahu. None of them moved a muscle to intervene. Elyahu even smiled

as he watched. When asked about it later, he said, 'I enjoyed watching Dina beaten and watching my wife realize what could be done to a woman who runs away from her husband. She will never run from me.' From this point on, the relationship between Shamca and Dina was a master-servant relationship.

Shamca realized that bullying and violence fit him well, both at home and in the chaikhans. He adopted a violent behavior pattern. Once, when his parents fought and his father hit his mother, Shamca chose to step in. He hit has father hard and broke several ribs. David lay in bed for a whole week, with Zere and Dina taking care of him. A year after their wedding, Shamca and Dina had their first son. All claims of Dina's inability to have a child were refuted. The son was named Fauzi, a name which attested to the Kurdish community's integration in the Iraqi community. Fauzi looked just like his father. He had brown-green eyes and smooth, light hair. When he was two years old, his sister Esther was born.

One day, when Fauzi was three years old, he was playing in the yard while Zere cooked peas on the primus stove. Shamca was at a chaikhan. Fauzi held a rubber snake and played with it. When a neighbor from another yard came by, he scared her with the snake.

'Ohhh,' screamed the woman jumping up in the air. 'You've become such a... I hope you burn,' she hissed and left.

While running in the yard, Fauzi accidently ran into the simmering pot and the hot beans spilled all over him. Hearing his screams, the neighbors stepped out of their homes - along with Dina. When they saw the boy's condition, they rushed him to the hospital. Dina lifted him onto her shoulders. Sarah joined her and together they ran to the nearest hospital - Majediyah, which was Muslim-owned. The Jews preferred the Jewish hospital, Meir Elias, but in Fauzi's condition there was simply no time to spare - they had to bring him to the

nearest hospital.

For three days little Fauzi struggled for his life. After three days he lost - and died.

For years, Dina blamed the hospital for his death. 'The burns weren't so bad. I've seen people with far worse burns who survived. I'm sure had he been a Muslim boy they would have treated him better.' She never stopped agonizing about not taking him to the Jewish hospital. 'They would have taken better care of him there,' she lamented. 'The Muslim doctors at Majediyah had no motivation to properly treat a Jewish boy.'

After Fauzi's death, Dina shut off. Her lust for life was gone. Zere, of all people - the one who saw Fauzi as the continuation of the family name - tried to calm her and coax Dina out of her depression. Whether this was done out of love and care, or in the hope that Dina could be encouraged to have another child, Zere gave her warmth and support, and saw her through her toughest hour.

Life in Baghdad was getting harder and harder. Alongside the violence at home, was the fear of violence on the street. After the establishment of the State of Israel, hatred for Jews grew stronger. The government in Baghdad and some fundamentalist organizations, incited the population against the Jews.

Finally, the Iraqi authorities decided to banish all Jews from the country. They had to turn over all their property - their money and their homes - and wait for their turn to leave. Mame, who was working for the childless couple, had already completed three years of work. Her elderly employer treated her like her own daughter. She taught her to sew, knit and weave. She also suggested Mame change her name to Rivka, explaining that Mame was a Muslim name whereas Rivka was her own mother's name, as well the name of one of Judaism's 'four mothers'.
'The name Rivka, like the biblical Rivka, is a better fit for a beautiful girl like you,' she said.
Mame took to the idea and adopted the name, which she liked a lot. Her new name quickly caught on in the family, too. Aside from her parents and her brother Shamca, everyone called her Rivka - and they still do.
Mame learned well all the things her employer taught her. The old woman's nephew would visit his aunt often. He was two years older than Mame. One day, when the woman heard that Mame wanted to move to Israel, she called her in and asked her to stay.
'I'll adopt you as my own daughter,' she told her. 'You can marry my nephew.'
'My mother will never agree,' said Mame.
'I'll pay your mother your weight in gold. You know that money is no problem for me.'
Mame went to her mother and told her of the offer. Zere was horrified. 'I wouldn't sell you for all the fortune in the world,' she exclaimed.

The next day Zere and Mame went together to see the lady. 'I know you want to go to Israel,' she told Zere. 'One day I go there myself. I just have to sell my property, get on a plane, and fly to Israel or London; I can take Mame with me. She can marry my nephew and they'll have a happy life together. We can always come visit you in Israel, even if we end up staying in London.'
Zere refused. She had already lost five children, and that was more than enough. What's more, she had never heard of London and had no idea where it was. 'That's all I need right now, for someone to take my child away to London...' she mumbled to herself. Since the woman kept trying to convince her, Zere promised to consult with her husband and get back to her. Zere and Mame left the house for the very last time; they never returned.
My family, just like everyone else, signed up for immigration. They had no property to give up, no houses, no plots of land. Knowing they would be searched when they boarded the plane, they got rid of all the jewelry and money they owned. They traded it for gold coins which they hoped to sneak into Israel. Sarah had a beautiful ring with a gold coin welded to it. Grib wanted to turn it into a wedding ring in the welders' market. Wedding rings were the only kind of gold which the inspectors did not confiscate at the airport. He took it and turned it into a wedding ring, and Sarah wore it on her finger - even though she wasn't married.
Grib was working for very rich people, the Jeda family. The head of the family, Naim, managed a worldwide commerce chain. Grib worked in the house. Apart from cleaning, he also tended the garden - a profession he specialized in - and ran various errands.
One day, after things in Iraq became very difficult, Naim called Grib in for a conversation. 'The atmosphere here is very bad,' he told him. 'You Kurds have it easier, but people like me, wealthy property owners - the Baghdad authorities are always looking for us. Have you noticed

how many people they've arrest recently? Have you seen how many people were hung in outskirts of town? I feel that my day will come soon, but before they get to me I plan to escape to London.

I have enough money to charter an airplane. I'll take with me only the things I can carry. Everything that can be sold, will be sold. I'll take small items, decorations, and expensive rugs that I keep at home. I plan on leaving this beautiful house as it is. Please take care of it until you leave - or perhaps until things calm down and I can return.'

Grib listened intently and then told Naim that he too had something he would like to smuggle out. 'I don't have tools and I'm not fleeing to London,' he said apologetically, 'Nor do I have any money for bribes, but I have two gold bracelets. One belongs to my wife and the other to my sister-in-law. These are very expensive bracelets - they are an amalgamation of everything we've managed to accumulate during our time here. These bracelets were made from gold coins. They are heavy and valuable. Take them, and God-willing, you will find the way to bring them back to me in Israel.'

'No problem,' replied Naim. 'Though I'm not traveling to Israel, I do have family there. I have a sister in Jerusalem. I'll find a way to return your bracelets.'

A few days later, Naim Jeda made true his plans. He paid whomever he needed to pay and managed to transfer some of his property to the plane via trucks crossing the roads of Baghdad. He and his entire family flew to London. Grib was left behind to take care of the house. He had nothing to take for himself - all that was left was the heavy furniture.

The idea of moving to the luxurious house never even crossed his mind. He was afraid someone might identify him as the owner of the house and kill him, since Kurds always tried to keep a low profile. Either way, he was planning on leaving Baghdad as soon as he had the chance.

"Not far from Khan Najab, where we lived, was a big school that was also used as a temple," Sarah described. "The school had a really big yard where the Iraqi government gathered all the Jews it wanted to deport - having first taken their property, of course. Every day, several planes (not Iraqi) would leave for Israel.

Each day around the school, they would announce the names of that day's travelers. We showed up every morning to find out whether or not it was our turn. One day they called our names. My mother, my father, Shamca and Dina with their daughter Esther, my sisters, and me. The Jews of Akra - Barkuna and his family included - had already left Iraq. When they departed, the search of travelers smuggling gold and silver was not as intense. As far as we knew, they managed to take along all their gold.

Hisne, her husband, and their three children, as well as Gado and his own family, left a few weeks after Barkuna. And now it was our turn.

Abd al Rahman was also named among the Jews who were deported from Iraq. Zere, David and Gado pleaded him to come to Israel with them, but he refused. He escorted them to the airport and promised to follow soon.

Upon boarding the airplane, we had to give away all our gold jewelry to the police. My family gave all their gold to Abd al Rahman in hopes that should he find a way to get to Israel, he would try and bring it along. Either way, they preferred that he keep the gold, rather than the Iraqi officers. In the end, he decided not to come to Israel - he went back to Akra and was never heard from again.

Jacob, one of Gado's sons, got married in Israel to a girl he had met in Akra - Geula. Her brothers, who lived in Tiberias, stayed in touch with some Jews in Akra who had converted to Islam, as well as some Christian friends. The connection was maintained mostly due to illegal travel via Turkey. On one of their trips, in 1955, they couldn't locate Abd al Rahman. When they inquired after him, they were told that he and his Muslim wife had been murdered by members of her family. This was while Mustafa Barzani escaped to the USSR. Without his family's assistance or Barzani's protection, Abd al Rahman was helpless; he couldn't save himself from being murdered by his wife's family. That was the end for Abd al Rahman."

"**After the procedures and document-signing, and**

after they took our passports, they transferred us to the airport," recalled Sarah. "When we boarded the plane, they conducted a meticulous search of each of us, including a physical search. Men searched men and women searched women. We were forbidden to take anything valuable - all was confiscated by order of the Iraqi government. They opened our suitcases too, but not in the usual way. They ripped them apart using knives, in order to go through our clothes.

We left nothing behind. We arrived in Baghdad from Kurdistan, penniless. We left Baghdad just as we had arrived to it, penniless. I, who had worked for very rich people, saw what they would leave behind. You have no idea of the kinds of things they let go of... It's hard to even imagine...a whole world: fancy houses, hospitals, mansions, schools, temples, thousands of apartments, courtyards, businesses - I tell you, it was a whole world. During all those years we knew that the Jewish Iraqis controlled Baghdad, culturally speaking. We admired them - the way they welcomed us, the warmth they showed us. For us, they were the real saviors. We learned so much from them. They were far more educated than the Iraqi Arabs. They were the society's elite.
Throughout our escape path - from Barzani, through Harran and Akra, and all the way to Baghdad - the only thing that guided us and determined our next move, was hunger. During our nine years in Baghdad, we never knew hunger. Jews put us up in their homes, fed us at their tables, even paid our salaries. It's true we hadn't become rich, but at least we were never hungry. A person who has never been hungry in their life just doesn't understand the amazing feeling of being full.
One of the things that impressed me the most, was seeing - for the first time in my life - a couple dancing together at a party in one of the richer homes. It was a husband and wife, holding each other's arms and

dancing. I'd just never seen it before. In Kurdistan it was taboo - women never danced with men. Every occasion saw men dancing in circles of men, and women in circles of women. Men and women never touched each other. And here - seeing a couple hold each other in public, on the dance floor - something that for me should have been seen as immoral, suddenly felt so right, so complete and noble. What could possibly be more natural than a man and a woman holding each other? They called it dans, from the English 'dance'.

Even the way in which the Iraqi Jews spoke was different from the Arab way. There was mutual respect. The Arabic they spoke was of the highest level, and their manners were superb. Their businesses spread all over the world. I would often overhear phone conversations with people in China, India, Hong Kong and more; they worked with colleagues all over the world."

"On the airplane the Iraqi officers searched us

obsessively from head to toe," Sarah stated with restrained anger. "They checked our shoes, underwear, hats, kaffiyehs - everything they found: every ring, every bracelet, every necklace - they placed in their pockets. You could see the hate and greed in their eyes. I was more disgusted with them than ever before.

After the humiliating search, they stood, holding our passports, at the entrance to the plane and asked each person to state their name. When you told them your name, your passport was returned and you were able to board the airplane. Here, a most amazing thing happened. When my turn came, they asked for my name:
'Sarah,' I replied.
'You are not allowed to board,' they barked at me. 'Come with us.'
My family's attempts to convince them to leave me alone were useless. 'All of you, get on the plane and get right out of here,' they said sternly. 'She's coming with us.' My family had no choice - they boarded the plane, which took off minutes later. Only I stayed behind.
The reason for this was because my passport read "Zilpah" instead of Sarah. It must have been a clerical error. When I was asked for my name again and said 'Sarah', they asked if I was sure. I replied yes. They took me aside to try and get to the bottom of things. Once the mistake was found, they sent me back home and told me to fetch a new passport - a real one, not a fake one. They kept my own passport.
I didn't know where to go. I thought I might return to the school yard to see if I could correct the mistake. Going home was not an option, since the room was already taken by Muslims.
It was a cold, dark night and I was wearing only a thin dress. I walked to the school. The yard was empty and there was no one there to speak with. I sat on the stairs

and decided to spend the night, awaiting morning. But after a while, when I saw the types of people who were hanging around there, I decided to walk to Reyna's house, which was only 15 minutes away.

When I arrived, I knocked but no one answered. I knocked again, louder. It was a two-story house and Reyna usually spent her time on the top floor. Again, no one answered the door. I knocked even louder. A neighbor who heard my knocking glanced out her window, so I walked over and knocked on her door. She opened it and told me that Reyna wasn't home - that she had fallen ill and been taken to the hospital.

'Which hospital?' I asked, in a worried tone.

'The British hospital,' she replied.

'Do you know where it is?'

'Yes - it's at the end of Al Rasheed street, in the Kumbhar Ali neighborhood.'

I panicked. Throughout my entire ten years in Baghdad, I had never once dared to enter that area. The one time I visited there was by mistake, when we had just arrived to town. Even then, the little I had seen of the neighborhood scared me to death. Hundreds, maybe even thousands of people were walking side by side. They were stomping their feet and hitting themselves until they bled. They were in ecstasy. They called out unintelligible words in a monotonous rhythm, something that sounded like 'Allah... Allah...'; I'd never seen a more frightening sight in my life.

That day, I escaped the street and went straight to Elo's house. I told him in detail everything I had seen. My fear must have been apparent. He smiled and explained that it was the "Day of Ashura".

'It's a Shiite memorial day,' he informed me. 'When I arrived here, two years before you, I also encountered this strange phenomenon. Just like you, I didn't understand what was going on. I was told about an Islamic sect called the Shiites and about this ceremony

of theirs. Since then I've never gone back.'"

About 1,400 years ago. the prophet Muhammad passed away. According to Islamic tradition, he was the last prophet, which meant that no one could take his place - particularly since he never appointed a successor. His followers needed a leader, so Muslims had to choose a man who would head the Islamic State as the prophet's representative on earth. But this person could not be a prophet, only a replacement - so they called him Khalifat Rasul Allah: the successor of Allah.

All the Muslims agreed on the first successor, Abu Bakr, and on the second one, Umar ibn Al-Khattab. But the third one was the source of many disputes. Some supported a respectable man from the Umayya family named Uthman; others supported Ali, Muhammad's cousin who grew up with him and was married to his daughter Fatima. This disagreement grew into a real war within Islam. It ended temporarily with the victory of Uthman, who became caliph, but the people who supported Ali did not accept his leadership. Not long after, Uthman was murdered by Ali's followers.

After the murder, Ali became caliph. People who supported the Umayya family believed that the caliph should come from their own branch, so Ali was murdered shortly after. His supporters traveled south, moving towards Saudi Arabia. They divided themselves from their Muslim brothers and established a new sect. The Arabic word for sect is shia; since then they have been known as the Shiites.

The war between the two sects intensified. Among the fighters was Husayn, Ali's son. He was killed in a fight in the city of Karbala, near Baghdad. In fact, Husayn was Muhammad's true biological heir, and his favorite grandson. He died on the tenth day of the month of Muharram, the first month in the Islamic calendar. That's why the memorial day is called Ashura (tenth), a day when Shiites mourn the death of Muhammad's

grandson, Husayn ibn Ali. They hit themselves until they bleed in a mass march and in a steady rhythm: that's what Sarah witnessed that day.

"The neighborhood was infamous," Sarah explained,

remembering everything as if it happened yesterday. "It was a bad neighborhood, full of dark southerners who harassed strangers. It was full of crime. Murders were a trivial matter, especially the murder of Jews. But I had no choice. I started walking towards it. I walked the entire length of Al Rasheed Street, Baghdad's main thoroughfare. I was afraid to ask anyone where the hospital was - I didn't want to be recognized by my Kurdish accent - particularly the Jewish elements of it. I was even more frightened of talking to the young people that hung out there. They were standing together and laughing in an intimidating way. I tried talking to the women, mostly the older ones.

Everyone knew how to direct me towards Kumbhar Ali. All I now needed to know was the exact location of the hospital. Once I arrived in the neighborhood, I walked slowly and quietly as so not to draw attention. Luckily, I ran into a very old man who noticed I was lost.
'What are you looking for, daughter?' he asked in fluent Arabic. I was 25 at the time, tall and white - a detail which drew a lot of attention from men and teenage boys.
'The British hospital,' I replied.
He explained in detail where the hospital was, and what the building looked like. When I arrived, I saw a large, beautiful gate, and two dark skinheads standing at the entrance. They stood as still as statues. At first, I thought they were statues. When I came closer, one of them moved heavily towards me.
'What do you want?' he asked me in Arabic laced with a British accent.
'I'm looking for Madam Reyna,' I answered.
'We are only guards, we don't know the patients,' he replied. He opened the gate about half a meter wide, stuck in his head, and called to one of the nurses. I peeked through the opening. I saw a big, round yard,

around which was a structure with many porches. On one of the porches appeared a dark woman in a nurses uniform.

'He turned to her and said, 'There's a woman here looking for Madam Reyna.'

'She's asleep,' the nurse replied. 'We can't wake patients at this hour.'

'Tell her Sarah is looking for her,' I yelled. 'I have to talk to her.'

'Wait here,' she said and disappeared back into the room. A minute or two later she came out again and instructed the guards to let me in. 'Come in through this door here and climb up to the second floor.'

I did as I was told and met the nurse on the stairs. She pointed the way to Reyna's room. When I entered, I found her leaning against a pillow and holding a newspaper. When she saw me, she put it aside, spread out her arms and began shouting happily,

'Sarah, how wonderful! You've decided to stay! You won't leave me, will you?'

I walked over to her. We hugged at length and I told her everything that had happened to me. 'I really want to leave, but there's a problem,' I said and went on to tell her about the passport mix-up, the school yard, and how I had no one to turn to and nowhere to sleep.

'I'm so scared,' I said, choking with tears. 'The atmosphere in Baghdad is so threatening, especially for Jews.'

'Reyna smiled. 'Remember how scared we were that night?' she asked.

'Of course I do,' I answered. We began to discuss the scary night to which she was referring: I was working as a cook for Reyna. She loved Kurdish food: kubbeh, yaprach, stuffed intestines. She particularly loved it when I made hingryia, a sweet and sour dish made of eggplant and tomatoes, similar to Greek Moussaka.

One night, when all of Reyna's Jewish houseworkers

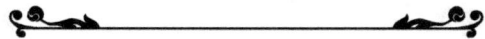

were either on vacation or headed to Israel, she was left on her own. Only I remained. I slept on the second floor. Suddenly we heard noises coming from the bottom floor. They sounded like the steps of someone walking in the dark and hitting the furniture, as if they were looking for their way. Reyna held me tight.

'They're coming to kill us, daughter,' she cried, her voice shaking. 'The Farhud is starting again.'
'I'll go take a look,' I suggested.
'No, no...' whispered Reyna. 'Don't go there, they'll kill you. But how did they get in? Everything is locked.'
'I'm going downstairs to see,' I said again.
'Fine, but take this flashlight.'
I took the flashlight and went down the stairs barefoot. At first, I looked around without turning the flashlight on. I knew the bottom floor well, even in utter darkness - I knew the location of each and every little thing. The noises hadn't stopped, but they no longer sounded like a person. They were ticking noises, and not particularly uniform ones. Since I knew no one was there, I turned the flashlight on and walked over to the source of the noise.
Surprisingly, it was a kite. It was making noises and stumbling onto furniture with every light breeze.
The children in Baghdad loved to play with kites. They would fly them high, and occasionally one of them would fall to the ground. This one must have fallen right through Reyna's open window. I took it in my hands and the room went quiet again. I turned to climb back up the stairs.
'Sarah, Sarah,' I heard Reyna say, choked up with fear.
'I'm coming up. Everything is fine, don't worry,' I assured her.
With a big smile - and the flashlight illuminating my face and the kite, I walked back into the room. 'That's all it was - a kite.'

Back at the hospital, the two of us burst into laughter remembering the story. We sat and chatted for an hour, Reyna trying to convince me to stay and not go back to Israel. 'You know me well,' she said. 'You know I work for the aliyah. Let me finish my work here and I promise you, in less than a year we will move to Israel together.'
'I can't,' I told her. 'My parents, brother and sisters are all in Israel. They must be worried and waiting for me. If I don't make it there in the next few days they will go crazy with worry. My parents have already lost five children. I have to board a plane to Israel the first chance I get.'
'And you will - but be patient,' Reyna replied. 'We'll go together. I'll set you up in Israel.'
'Reyna,' I suddenly burst out, raising my voice, 'I'm moving to Israel!'
When she realized that I'd made up my mind, she took a set of her house keys and gave them to me. 'Here you go. Sleep over at my house and tomorrow morning return them to me. Then you can go to the school yard,' she instructed. 'You can use my clothes. Take whatever you want, wear whatever you want, pack whatever you want... Good luck.'
I took the keys, gave her a long kiss, and walked to her house.
Despite the darkness, I still tried to return to her house unnoticed. I locked the door behind me and went right up to the second floor. I couldn't sleep a wink the whole night. With only my dress on, I stepped onto the porch and sat down to look at the street below. It had quite a lot of traffic - cars and buses driving soldiers around.
All night long I sat on that porch. I didn't cry, though I was afraid of what the next day might bring. What will happen in the school yard? Will they call my name? Will the mistake be corrected? Am I destined to stay in exile, while my entire family is in Israel?"
Early in the morning, before sunrise, I left the house.

I didn't take anything with me; I didn't even change my clothes. I only put on my shoes and headed to the hospital to see Reyna.

The guards recognized me and let me in. I returned Reyna's keys and said my last goodbye, probably forever. I now needed to go back to the school yard. I decided to follow Reyna's advice: 'Scream! Don't give up!' she instructed me.
The school yard was overflowing with people. I went up to the officials who were in charge of reading out the names. 'All of the names are right here on the wall,' they showed me. 'If you can spot your name, stand where it's written.'
'But I can't read,' I exclaimed. 'And there are no photos!'
'Oh, you want photos too?' they mocked me.
'I already boarded the plane,' I told them. 'They took me off because of your mistake.'
'Well, we're not dealing with special cases right now. Step aside and when we get to the special cases, we will handle yours.'
I stayed in that yard for three days. I didn't dare go back to Reyna, fearing she might talk me into staying in Iraq. I found a corner and spent the night there. During the day, I spent my time trying every possible way to get the officials to notice me and help solve my problem. I hardly had anything to eat during that time. The other Jews in the yard offered me some dates and fruit, but I had no appetite. I was wallowing in fear; I was afraid I would have to spend the rest of my life in exile, without a family.
Three days later, the official in charge stepped up to me. 'Here is your passport, Zilpah,' he said. 'And that's how it will remain: Zilpah. That is your new name. If you want to leave for Israel you will have to do so with your new name.'
I took the passport and joined the group that was

preparing to leave for the airport. I had nothing at all, apart from the thin dress I was wearing. The weather was freezing - this all happened in March, at the end of winter. There was an advantage to it though, no one could search me or my nonexistent belongings. When I arrived at the airplane, I recalled what I had been through only three days earlier. I couldn't bear to relive it. I almost lost my breath when one of the clerks came up to me, 'What is your name?' he asked.

'Zilpah,' I replied.

Before I came to my senses, I found myself sitting on the airplane in a seat by the window. The deafening noise scared me. I'd never flown anywhere before. The plane was so cold, and I was shivering from cold and excitement. When we took off, I felt terrified and confused.

After a while I began to vomit. There wasn't much room on the plane, and I felt bad. Suddenly I felt a hand on my shoulder. I turned to look and there was Isaac, one of Reyna's cleaning workers. 'Kaibrd lek?' he asked me in Iraqi Arabic, meaning: Are you cold?' I nodded.

He brought me a little blanket and a cloth with which to clean my dress. I wrapped myself in the blanket. It was so small it hardly covered my shoulders, but I felt a little bit better, perhaps also thanks to seeing a familiar face. The plane flew the entire night. As we were getting ready to land, commotion began. 'We've arrived in the land of Israel,' everyone cried. I was weak and thin. When I got off the plane and stepped on the land, I bent down to kiss the soil. I leaned in so fast that I fell on my face. Several people came to my assistance.

'Leave me for a moment,' I asked and kissed the ground. A minute later I got up. All I could see were dark circles. The land was slipping beneath my feet and the whole world was turning... Now all I had to do was find my family, I thought - but a moment later I collapsed again. The people who were holding me spoke a mixture of

Arabic and Hebrew. These were members of the Jewish Agency for Israel, whose job it was to welcome us to the country. They sat me down on a chair and offered me some water. An official from the aliyah agency arrived as well, urging us to leave, as the train was about to depart.

I became anxious. I had imagined that when I landed I would be greeted by my family, all waiting for me at the airport. Now I was afraid to get on the train: who knew where it would take me and whether I'd ever see my family again. I felt like they were somewhere near the airport, while I was being taken away, to who knows where.

'What about our luggage?' some people began yelling. 'We have luggage on the plane.'

'Your luggage will join you on the train,' the agency men shouted back.

We boarded the train. It was a cargo train heading north. On the way, it stopped and some volunteers boarded, carrying crates of fresh oranges. They gave each of us an orange. When the train stopped, we were told that we had arrived at a place called Sha'ar Ha'Aliya. When we got off the train, we were each given a matzah, in celebration of Passover.

I had never tasted an Israeli matzah before; It was hard and fragile. In Kurdistan, we used to make them ourselves - they were a type of bread we would bake on the saj. They tasted different, and had a different texture back home. I didn't like how the Israeli matzah tasted, but I had to eat something to keep from collapsing. After eating the matzah and the orange, I felt a little stronger. Sha'ar Ha'Aliya, Hebrew for "The Aliyah Gate", was supposed to be a transit camp, for stays lasting up to one week. But the more people that arrived, the longer they had to stay. Officials from border control examined each person's documents. Agency members wrote down our details and doctors examined us. About a thousand people went through these examinations every day. Everyone went through sterilization: we were told to get undressed and then sprayed with DDT. We were then moved to other camps where we might stay for weeks, or even months.

The camp was diverse and colorful. Some people wore suits, as was customary in central Europe; others wore the white robes of North African Jewry; and some were wearing flat caps or covering their heads in floral scarves. There was a wide diversity of people - all ages, from all over the world: awkward and confused, dragging suitcases, boxes and bags, and running around in a big commotion, surrounded by many, many babies and children who were screaming in every imaginable language.

Each person who arrived at the camp received food stamps, as well as two blankets and a piece of soap. Then he or she was sent to find an unoccupied bed.

The camp was almost completely full, and it was hard to find free space. The place consisted of several structures, long halls covered with tin roofs. Before the State of Israel was established, these were used by the British Army; there were also a few tents available for use.

The camp was full of clothing items and kitchen utensils. Many of the camp dwellers just sat on their beds all day with nothing to do. The air smelled of decay and rot. Children ran around between the beds. Many of the immigrants ate in the sleeping halls, and some cooked their meals themselves. There was a dining room in the camp, but it had no knives, forks or spoons, so diners had to eat with their bare hands. We were always hungry, as the food did not really satisfy, and no one knew how long they would have to stay there.

"Those were very tough days for us all," Sarah told me. "We had to go through a whole process which included getting sorted by family and country of origin. We were

sprayed with DDT. The whole thing just went on and on. One day, as I was sitting on a little stool, I looked up and suddenly saw Grib.

I collapsed again. He picked me up along with the help of a few other people who were present. He sat me on a stool and, in Arabic, told the agency officials that he was there to pick me up.

'That's not possible,' they informed him. 'She has to go through the entire immigration process, just like you did.'

'Well then, I'd like to take her for a short while, just so her family and her parents can see her,' said Grib. 'I promise I'll bring her right back.'

The agency officials smiled and immediately arranged a truck and a driver. He took us to Kfar Tavor, about half an hour's drive from Atlit, where we had arrived on the train. During the drive, all I could think about was Hisne, and what a wonderful sister she was. She must have sent Grib to me, I thought. Hisne never had to utter a word - all she had to do was look at Gribo and he knew just what she wanted. She had real magical powers over him.

We arrived at Kfar Tavor and I finally had the chance to see my parents, brother and sisters. It was a short meeting, since the driver urged us to go back. Grib returned with me and stayed in the camp with me for a while. 'Everything will be just fine,' he said as we parted. 'We're waiting for you.'

I remained on my own in Atlit. After finishing the immigration process I was taken to Kfar Tavor with a small group of people who were also assigned there. We rode in an open truck. The driver tried to tell us about all the places we were driving by, almost yelling in the attempt to overcome the engine noise and the wind. I tried to listen carefully, but apart from the name Afula - which he said as we were passing a town along the way - I didn't catch a thing.

On the other hand, I'll never forget the sight that unfolded before my eyes. It was March, and spring was in full bloom. The green I saw around me filled my eyes and my heart. The blossoms were beautiful. Through the tears, which were washing my face, I could see the most gorgeous landscape I'd ever witnessed. My God, I said to myself, I'm in the land of Israel... I'm in paradise."
The year was 1951. The young State of Israel had opened

its gates to immigration, "aliyah". Jews from all over the world wanted to make aliyah. More than 900,000 people moved to Israel in the first decade of its existence. That is a record, an unprecedented feat no matter how you look at it; it has no equivalence anywhere in the world. The dramatic increase in population within such a short period of time - along with the shifting ratio between veterans and new immigrants - meant that the country needed new institutional solutions and fast.

Between 1948-1949, the country's population grew by 28.3%. The next year saw a 16.7% rise and the next, 15.2%. The immigrants were initially housed in aliyah camps or transit camps. The quick increase in arrivals, the crowding, and the harsh conditions forced the state to come up with an alternative solution.

Levi Eshkol, Treasurer and Head of the Settlements Division of the Jewish Agency, had to find a quick solution for taking care of the new immigrants and their housing crisis. Eshkol worked systematically to make homes for tens of thousands of immigrants in abandoned Arab villages. At the same time, he encouraged the establishment of dozens more new settlements.

As the immigration wave expanded, various state officials - Eshkol among them - realized that the solutions they currently employed to handle the expanding population, could not solve the immigrant housing issue, or their other problems. In fact, the policies further encouraged the financial dependence of the immigrants on government assistance.

The British army camps and the hastily-built immigration camps were soon full to capacity. The cost of maintenance and the expenditure per capita, including administrative costs, was about one Israeli Lira per day. This expense took a heavy toll on the young state.

That's when Levi Eshkol came up with a new plan - to set up immigrant neighborhoods near older towns all over the country. His vision was to establish a new form of settlement, which was later called a "ma'abara", Hebrew for transit. The basic idea behind the ma'abarot was to provide the immigrants with jobs in established towns, and eventually to merge the city and the new settlement.

Another solution for the economic dependency was to set up government-initiated projects. The state believed that building ma'abarot around the periphery of the country would create a more balanced residential dispersion, which in turn, would help the country's security. Eshkol's plan was quickly put into motion. By May of 1950, the very first ma'abara was established in the Jerusalem mountains area. The main difference between a transit camp and the ma'abara concerned the immigrants' responsibility for their own livelihood. In the transit camps, they received food and housing free of charge; in the ma'abara they had to work and support themselves.

Once the family was reunited, a new problem emerged. The world they had left behind, one which they knew

so well, died at once. The new world they were facing was cold and alienating. They did not speak Hebrew well. Their professions in Baghdad: housekeeping, cleaning, laundry, cooking, running errands, and so on, did not demand they speak Hebrew, so they again found themselves with no livelihood, no food, and without the ability to communicate.

'Daarakh hawa,' said David: We will go back.
Zere shot him a threatening look. 'To where exactly do you want to return?' she asked, enraged. 'They've deported us and told us if we ever come back they will kill us. Where do you want to go? We've spent all our lives dreaming about Israel, and now that we're here you want to leave?'
'But what will we eat?' asked David. 'This is on you now. The responsibility is on your shoulders. Take care of food for the entire household.'
And, indeed, the women all went out to work in the surrounding farms. They picked cucumbers, tomatoes and anything else that grew. Sarah and Dina, now 25 years old, became best friends. They went to work together plucking poultry. Dina would leave little Esther - now one year old - with grandmother Zere, and go to work.
Shamca had too much energy to stay at home, and he also began searching for work. Everytime he left the ma'abara, he noticed minarets in the distance. He realized that there were Arabs around, who spoke his language. He made his way towards the mosques, and that's how he found himself in nearby Arab villages like Daburiyya, Shibli and Sejera. He entered the villages and walked around in the alleys. He soon found the markets, and more importantly, his beloved chaikhans.
Happily, they were just like the chaikhans he knew back in Baghdad: the same tables, the same dominoes and card games, the same wooden stools... He was

particularly pleased to find the familiar image of the hookah-smoking Arabs playing backgammon, just like in Baghdad. He stared at them for several minutes, contemplating how to approach them. Finally, one of the men noticed him. The man walked up to him and in fluent Arabic asked, 'Are you looking for someone?'
'No,' Shamca replied. He noticed that the man's Arabic was different from the Iraqi dialect he knew from back home. 'I've come from Iraq,' he said in Iraqi Arabic. 'I live in a ma'abara in Kfar Tavor. I saw the mosques from far away and decided to come see who lives here. I've only been here a short while, I don't speak Hebrew... When I saw the mosques, I knew I could find someone to communicate with here.'
'You speak well,' the man told him. 'That must be Iraqi Arabic.'
'It is,' answered Shamca. 'I've come from Baghdad.'
'Sit down,' said the local to Shamca. 'Have a glass of tea - it's on me.' The two sat and chatted in Arabic. Shamca didn't like card games, but he knew and loved dominoes. So Shamca would arrive every day to the chaikhans in the Arab villages, play his dominoes, drink his tea, talk to the locals and feel right at home, as if someone copied Baghdad and placed it in Israel.
Gradually, more and more Jews from the ma'abara and other distant towns joined in. One day, two Jews came along whom Shamca knew back in Akra. These men did not pass through Baghdad, they must have immigrated to Israel straight from Akra. Shamca recognized them right away, and they recognized him. They all hugged and kissed and each told his own story - what had happened to him since they last saw each other in 1942.
After a few weeks, Shamca began feeling comfortable in his new environment, like he had in Baghdad, where he intervened in fights in order to solve them, particularly when honor was on the line. Once, two of his friends from Akra got into a fight in the cafe. Shamca rose up

and without hesitation, punched the man who was fighting them. Unfortunately, that man was wearing glasses. The punch was so hard that it broke his nose as well as the glasses, causing a large cut on his face.

Shamca thought that he had solved the problem and brought back the peace, just like he used to do in Baghdad. He never considered things worked differently in Israel. Within minutes the police arrived. They handcuffed him and took him to the police station in Tiberias. On the way, he began feeling pain in his thumb, which he probably fractured when he threw the punch. The policemen saw him holding his fingers and realized he was also injured. After they processed his arrest, they took him to a local doctor in order to fit his finger in a cast. Shamca didn't know what a cast was; he was sure they were going to cut off his finger. When he got back to his cell he ripped the cast off off with his teeth, and threw it in the corner.

While he was gone, his friends returned from the ma'abara and told Dina that her husband had been arrested.

Meanwhile, Grib and Gado were living in a tent camp in Tiberias. Barkuna, who arrived shortly before them and managed to bring with him all the gold he had back in Kurdistan, did not live there. He bought himself some land with a couple of sheds. He would eventually become one of the wealthiest men in Tiberias, but like his father Moshe, he would never share his riches with his brothers. And just like his father before him, he lived by the Arabic saying, "inta washatartak", meaning: you and your own wit.

When Dina got word of Shamca's arrest, she wanted to see him. She could think of no other way to get to Tiberias, except the tried-and-true method of walking. Even several days of walk seemed trivial to her, and the distance between Kfar Tavor and Tiberias was only half a day's walk. She placed her daughter Esther on her back, and began walking.

When she reached Tiberias, she asked around to find out where the immigrants were staying. She soon reached Hisne's tent and told her what had happened.

'What can we do to help?' asked Hisne.

'Only one thing,' replied Dina. 'I want to cook food with your help, to take to Shamca every day until he is released.'

Dina and her child moved into the Tiberias tent camp. Every day, she and Hisne would make stew which Dina would take to the police station. A week later, Shamca was released. They made their way back to the ma'abara by foot.

A few days later, Zere told Dina something in secret.

'I know,' Dina told her. I also think it's time. But we have a problem - there's no mikveh here for me to dip in and become pure. There's no river or spring, no source of water at all...'

'You'll find a way,' said Zere.

When evening came, Dina grabbed a large container, filled it with water, and wearing nothing but her nightgown, went behind the row of sheds, swung the bucket with all her might, and in one move, poured the water onto her head and body. That was a good cleansing, she thought to herself, now I'm allowed to have more children.

"We stayed in the ma'abara for several months," Sarah told me. "One day representatives from the Jewish

Agency arrived and told us we had to leave. We wanted to move to Tiberias to be with our family - Hisne, Grib and Barkuna - but we were told there was no more room. They began suggesting other towns: Kiryat Shmona, Hatzor, Betzet... places we've never even heard of."

When we were in exile we used to dream of Jerusalem, Tiberias and Hebron, holy cities which are mentioned in the holy texts and in prayers. In later years we also heard about Tel Aviv and Ramat Gan. We heard so many strange names that we knew nothing about.
Sarah tried hard to remember the other towns that were suggested to them.
'Well, if Tiberias has no more room and Hebron is not a part of Israel anymore, we want to go to Jerusalem,' we told the Agency members.
'Do you have any relatives or friends in Jerusalem? Or anywhere in Israel at all?' they asked.
'We do,' I told them. 'About 20 years ago, some people came to Israel from Akra and Barzan. They are a part of our family. Their names are Shimon and Moshe Barzan and they live in Jerusalem. If it's at all possible, we would love to move there.'
'No problem,' the agency representatives replied, 'but you will have to do it yourself.'
'Meaning?'
'Meaning you'll have to find a car to take you there on your own,' they explained. 'And try to do it as fast as you can, because we need the space - many more immigrants are coming and we need to help them settle here.'
Our neighbors from Akra, who arrived to Israel shortly before we did, had already familiarized themselves with life in this country. They helped us find a truck and a driver named Isaac. We all pitched in and paid the little money we had earned from our work on the farm.
We got on the truck and headed to Jerusalem. When we

neared the city we were dropped off at an abandoned Arabic village called Lifta, right at the entrance to town. The villagers abandoned it during the Arab-Israeli war of 1948, on orders from the Arab High Committee. They were hoping to return to it once the war was over and the Jews were removed.

The village was built on a hillside and the houses stood on the edges of caves. These were real ruins, full of donkey and goat droppings. Each family had to find a house and settle in. The entire family - David and Zere, Sarah, Ruhama and Rivka, and Shamca, Dina and Esther - found a potential home in one old and long structure. Since they were no longer in an immigration camp and there was no longer any free food available, they needed to find work and start earning a living. No agriculture was done in the region, which was very different from the settlements near Kfar Tavor, which were located in the fruitful Jezreel Valley. They had no choice but to go back to doing housework, like they had done in Baghdad.

Up the mountain from Lifta was a narrow path that lead to Jerusalem. The neighborhoods that bordered Lifta were Givat Shaul, Kiryat Moshe and Beit Hakerem. In the Rehavia neighborhood, a little farther from the village, lived more wealthy Jews who had been living in Israel for many years.

"We walked there in order to offer our services," Sarah remembered. "We spoke Arabic; surprisingly, many of them did too. We all managed to find housework in the rich houses of Rehavia. We had to make the walk every day from our house in Lifta to a place called Emeq Ha'arazim, then to the top of the mountain and the road leading to Rehavia.

It would take us an hour-and-a-half every morning. We would go in groups, singing together, 'We have a job, God is good / we'll take the money and buy us food / wait a few moments with your group / for pickled fish and

some vegetable soup / we can't afford no cigarettes / but we have a job, God is great...' Our song became a real hymn and we would sing it over and over again.

Dina was already five months pregnant. A month later, Grib showed up at our door in Lifta and told us he had left Tiberias. 'We've left my brothers and have come to live in Jerusalem,' he said. 'We live here, on the top of the mountain. Now we're real neighbors.'

Grib, who had a particularly good sense of orientation, was happy to finally be in Jerusalem. He and Gado used to hike all over the Kurdistan mountains, and they could navigate using the sun and the moon - but mostly by using their intuition. The valley he could see from our home in Lifta was remarkably similar to the view in Barzan. The same houses on the hillside, the same orchards full of fruit trees such as pomegranates, almonds, grapes, and strawberries. The same water spring, the same mountains... He felt at home. Grib would hike the mountains, hills, and valleys all day long. He examined every corner, every tree, every plant. He knew how to find food in the ground."

Grib and Hisne had three children: Moshe, who was eight; Naji, who was six, and Ruti was one-and-a-half. For the children, the valley was a real paradise. They studied every nook and cranny. They knew the trees, the paths, the flora, the houses; they knew where each person lived. Most of all, they loved the water spring, where they spent many hours of the day dipping their toes and swimming.

Following Grib, Gado arrived a few weeks later. He left Tiberias, so Barkuna's family remained by themselves.

He also searched for a place to live on the Lifta hillside. Up the hill, next to the road that the villagers used for traveling to work every morning, he found a structure which was very long, but horribly dirty. It must have been used for housing livestock. It was in ruins, but Gado and his sons cleaned it well.

When they were done, he made Shamca an offer. 'Leave your parents,' he suggested, 'and come live with me - you, your wife and your daughter. Our house is big enough. We can partition it using a curtain and there will be enough space for us all.' Shamca happily accepted and the family moved in with Gado.
A few months passed. The women worked in the households of the rich residents of Rehavia. They also had to walk down to the spring to fetch water, do laundry, and cook for their men, who did very little apart from hiking - at least for a while.
"They were in shock," my mother Dina used to day. "It took them longer than it did us to get used to the change. We women immediately took over everything - we had no choice. We had a home to run, children to feed. In fact, the men were like children themselves."
On June 4th, 1952, a Wednesday, and a few months after her arrival at Lifta, Dina went into labor. She immediately walked over to her good friend and sister-in-law Sarah. 'My time has come to give birth,' she said. Sarah, who knew the area well, told her about a hospital that was located not to far away. It was called Wallach, or Sha'are Zedek. 'It's only an hour's walk,' she said.
The two held hands and began walking. They left Esther with her grandmother, Zere. It was lunchtime, and the sun was burning above them. Climbing the mountain was a difficult task. Sarah supported Dina the entire way. When they arrived at the top of the mountain, Dina felt like she was about to give birth right then and there.
They hurried to the path leading to the hospital. A few

minutes after their arrival, Dina gave birth to a baby boy. She made Zere's dream of giving Shamca a male descendent come true. Everyone was thrilled. Back then, they would name children after a king or a ruler - this was true in Iraq as well. Dina asked what the King of Israel was called. They explained to her that in Israel there is a president, not a king, and that his name was 'Weizmann'.

'Wezman?" she asked, embarrassed. "I don't like that name...'

Along with her mother-in-law Zere, she decided to name the boy Isaac, after Zere's uncle who was murdered in Barzan. Six months later, on December 1952, President Chaim Weizmann passed away and Yitzhak Ben-Zvi became the second president of the State of Israel. 'There," said Dina to Zere, 'we wanted a president and got one... All in God's will.'

We spent two-and-a-half years in Lifta. Having lived in Baghdad and gotten used to electricity, running water, house doors and so on, the family felt like it was going back in time, as if they were in Barzan again. In Lifta we lived in caves, in ruined structures with no doors, which leaked from the walls and roofs in the winter. We brought water from the spring, collected wood to make a fire, burned it in the houses in winter, and outside the houses in summer. Three years we lived like that, in substandard conditions, without any government service paying us any attention. Those were our first steps in the country.

Why did Kurdistan Jews keep silent about the injustice they suffered? Why didn't they rise and protest like the

people of Wadi Salib in Haifa or the Black Panthers in Jerusalem? Probably because of their unique character, Kurdish Jews never look back, but always forward.

Their individualistic nature and survival instincts are responsible for their ability to start anew every time. Just like they did when escaping Barzan and needing to start over in every new place, they did the same in Israel. They never looked back or returned to their origins. They pulled themselves up by their bootstraps and without any outside help, built their future in their new country.
Just look around to see how well this community managed to integrate into Israel's economy: in construction, settlement, agriculture and more. Most dirt and construction contractors in Jerusalem are Kurdish. Most of the country's agricultural settlements, about which we hardly ever hear but which have flourished as amazing farming achievements, are populated by Kurds. Most builders are Kurds. They were among the first stonemasons, porters, Jewish construction workers, quarry workers, paving workers.
In our family, we made a point of always being in charge of our own destiny. The first one to realize that we had to make do on our own was Gribo. After receiving some advice from a friend at work, he went in search of houses among the lost properties of nearby neighborhoods. He found a two-bedroom home in Givat Shaul, and moved into it with his wife and children. Gado followed his example. He left Lifta and moved in with Gribo in the same yard, in another room.
'Now it's time for us to also leave Lifta,' said Dina. After everyone else left, we knew we had to follow. What little money we managed to save in our two-and-a-half years of work was not enough to buy a house. Then we learned about the concept of "key money" - buying a house for a low price and paying rent to the owner for

the rest of your life. If you eventually sold the house, you had to give a third of the money to the landlord. In other words, you never actually own the property, and are forced to pay rent forever.

Shamca and Dina wanted to buy a room for key money. The money they had was enough to leave Lifta and move to a room on Hakishon street, in the Kurdish neighborhood of Jerusalem; the name has been changed since then; it is now known as Eliyahu Salman Street. David, Zere, and their daughters: Sarah, Rivka and Ruhama, had relocated near the Kurdish neighborhood even earlier. They lived in a shabby room on Korazin Street, in Sha'are Rahamim. The room had a tiled roof with no cement casting, so it leaked every winter. The bathroom, which was shared by the neighbors, was located on the bottom floor. The small kitchen had a water tap, but the water ran into a bucket which had to be emptied every time it was full.

During the years since leaving Baghdad, Sarah had been waiting for the return of the bracelet she had given to Gribo's employer to smuggle. Every time she visited Hisne and Gribo at their home in Givat Shaul, she hinted about it. Occasionally, she even dared ask the question, 'The bracelet's gone, isn't it?'

Three years passed. Gribo kept in touch with Naim's sister, who moved to Jerusalem shortly before Naim left for London. She and her husband were living on Betzalel Street, near the Prozinin Clinic. Gribo became friends with them and visited occassionally.

One morning in 1954, Gribo appeared at the little house in the Kurdish neighborhood, holding the bracelet. With a casual expression - just like the day he picked Sarah up from the immigrant camp - he handed her a small box with her long-lost bracelet inside. He gave a brief but meaningful smile, sat on the chair and asked, 'Can I have a glass of tea?'

Today, when I think about how they were thrown into Lifta with no electricity, no water, no sanitary

conditions and no medical aid, I feel I need to mention one more thing: during the early years, the State of Israel had to accommodate a lot of immigrants from all over the world; it was no easy task.

The first issue was housing. That was solved quickly enough by setting up the ma'abarot. While those isolated ma'abarot helped disperse the population across the country, it denied the immigrants proper integration, and made it difficult to find work. Only 98 ma'abarot were built near cities, while the other 31 were built far from any functioning settlement - Yeruham, for instance. The houses of the ma'abarot were very basic, having been built as a temporary solution. The most common of them were small sheds, tents, fabric-made sheds, sheds of asbestos, and tin houses. Many went to live in abandoned Arab villages, as was the case with Lifta, near Jerusalem.
Though the mass immigration during Israel's first three years of existence consisted primarily of travelers from Asia, North Africa, Europe, and America in almost equal parts, by 1952, Asian and North African immigrants made up over 80% of ma'abarot dwellers. Unlike their Asian and North African counterparts, immigrants from Europe and America almost miraculously found themselves outside the ma'abarot, integrated into veteran populations with proper homes and jobs. This ratio held throughout the years. The primary reasons include the discriminating policies of the offices in charge of settlement in Israel (headed by The Jewish Agency), and their disproportionate bias toward European and American descendents with regard to relocation in central Israel.
One example of this discrimination can be found in the protocol from a special meeting between The Jewish Agency and David Ben Gurion, in which Yehuda Braginsky, head of the Aliyah Division, reviewed the

immigration records up to 1956.

The protocol reads, "In the last 27 months, 85 thousand people made aliyah from North Africa and 85% were directed to developing regions outside the Gedera-Nahariya strip. They were sent to places such as Be'er Sheva, Dimona, Eilat, Ofakim, Azata, Kiryat Gat, Kiryat Shmona, Hatzor and Betzet. With the Polish immigration, things are different. In the last two months, more than 2,000 people immigrated from Poland. Some were placed in empty spaces within the Gedera-Nahariya strip, since some apartments remained vacant for us to use; we will send Polish immigrants to Zikhron Ya'akov and Binyamina, since we can't send them to live in sheds and fabric-made houses; they need a proper dwelling." Another factor was the quality of connections that native Israelis had with European and American Jews. These immigrants used their relationships with Israelis, mostly family members, to help them leave the ma'abarot.

Life in the ma'abarot took its toll, particularly on those living in the more isolated areas. They developed resentment, and felt they were being discriminated against, which led to a deep social tear between immigrants from Islamic states and those from Europe. In 1953 the ma'abarot started to disintegrate. Some of them fell apart spontaneously when residents relocated. Others were deliberately taken apart by the state in an attempt to turn them into a new kind of settlement. To the great surprise of Jewish Agency officials, some immigrant groups refused to leave the camps and chose to remain under the agency's patronage. In response, The Jewish Agency began using sanctions, halting the shipment of food and shutting down camp kitchens, all with the declared purpose of forcing the settlers to evacuate.

By the end of 1954, only 90,000 people still lived in the ma'abarot. Many other ma'abarot became new cities and

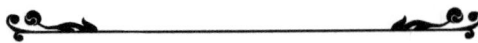

towns, such as Kiryat Malachi, Sderot, Beit Shemesh, Beit She'an, Kiryat Shmona and Yeruham. Still others became thriving neighborhoods within existing cities, such as Lifta, Talpiot, and Kastel. This was especially true for the Kastel ma'abara, which was populated mostly by Kurdish immigrants and eventually became Maoz Zion, a local council. In later years, it merged with neighboring council, Mevasseret Yerushalaym. Today the merge is called Mevasseret Zion, and it is one of the most prestigious residential regions in the area.

I can imagine the convoluted path taken by the Kurdistan Jewry from mountains and caves, all the while, doing their best to survive the pogroms and the hate. I think of the fear they must have lived through, the need to hide their Jewish identity and at the same time, live a full Jewish life, observe the Sabbath, the holidays, the tradition of brit milah, and so on. When I think of the humiliations they suffered and the money and property that was taken from them, I always slip back to the magical time of my own youth. What a wonderful childhood I had! All of us who were born and raised in Israel, poor as we were, tasted honey. We were happy and content with what we had; we had everything. We never had to live under foreign rule, nor suffer oppression or persecution.

There is one particularly special experience I remember from my childhood, an experience I can still enjoy today, on the steps in front of the Mahane Yehuda market in Jerusalem. It is a unique experience, unlike anything else in the world. I invite anyone who desires the experience to go to the market on a Friday afternoon. On Agripas Street is a gate to the Ohel Moshe neighborhood and a place called Gan Hatut - "strawberry garden" - the same one from Yossi Banai's song: "Me, Simon, and Little Moiz". This gate faces Ets Khayim Street, the main street of the market.

Sit on the steps and observe Ets Khayim Street: the

bustle of the market and the merchants yelling about their goods; watch the shoppers, the passers-by, one with bags and another with a shopping cart, and you'll understand that the Sabbath is about to come in. Now a magical process takes place. Slowly, the market quiets: shoppers decrease, and one store after another closes. Eventually, the merchants leave. When the market is empty, municipal workers appear with their water hoses to wash down the market.

All that remains - the leftover fruit and vegetables, the cardboard boxes - all is washed away down Agripas and Nisim Bachar Streets. In the crosswalk sits a giant dumpster, into which the cleaners place the trash. The water slowly disappears into drains by the sidewalk. The dumpster is taken away and the market is clean. Suddenly the entire place becomes absolutely silent.

I like sitting there, on the steps, during this process; I like to watch the whole event unfold, the noise turned into silence.

After a few minutes, men emerge from the alleys dressed in their finest Sabbath attire: white kippot, brown and grey caps, shirts of white, yellow, blue - all the colors of the rainbow, pressed trousers. Accompanied by their sons, who are dressed just as finely, they proudly walk to temple.

While watching them, I ask myself for the umpteenth time: Is this not deliverance itself? Are we really still waiting for Messiah? Didn't he arrive already, some 100+ years ago? Isn't this process that we've been going through for decades, deliverance? Isn't the fact that we live here, in the land of our forefathers, in peace and independence - is that not deliverance? Are we not upholding Zechariah's own prophecy? This is what the Lord Almighty says, "Once again, men and women of a ripe-old-age will sit in the streets of Jerusalem, each of them with cane in hand because of their age. The city streets will be filled with boys and girls playing there"

(Zechariah 8:4-5).
If this isn't deliverance realized, well then tell me what is...

Note

In the interest of full disclosure, I'd like to make something clear - the story of Grib and Barkuna's fight was told to me by Hisne. To be fair, I should have asked for a version of events from the other side, as well - in other words, I should have discussed it with Barkuna and Sarah. Unfortunately, by the time I wrote this book, they had both passed away. Their children were born after the fight took place, and that is why the story of the fight is told from a single perspective.

Hebrew - Aramaic/Barzan (Jewish) Dictionary

I've added a short dictionary to this book, with which I hope to teach the most basic words of the language: pronouns, possessives, prepositions, and the nouns regarding family, days of the week, numbers, and more. I would also like to address the issue of pronunciation of certain letters. For instance, the difference between a strong K and kh (Bar Kokhva). A similar difference exists between strong T and th.
It is important to note that the language, as a whole, is spoken in penultimate stress (kalba, not kalba).

Pluralization
In terms of the pluralization of nouns, nearly all nouns (plants, animals, etc..) end in some variation of the vowel 'a'. To make the word plural, turn the last vowel into an 'e'. For instance:
Head = resha; heads = reshe
Hand = yida; hands = yide
Dog = kalba; dogs = kalbe
Donkey = khamra; donkeys = khmare
Apple = khbusha; apples = khbushe
Plum = khuluka; plums = khuluchke
Family Members
Father = baba
Mother = yima
Brother = kona
Sister = kalnta
Maternal Uncle = kaloyia
Paternal Uncle = amoyia
Maternal Aunt = kalta
Paternal Aunt = amta
Maternal Male Cousin = bar kaloyia
Paternal Male Cousin = bar amoyia
Maternal Male Cousin = brat kaloyia

Paternal Female Cousin = brat amoyia
Brother-in-law = adma
Sister-in-law = yidamta
Father-in-law = kmayiana
Mother-in-law = kmaha

Pronouns
Me = ana
You = ati
He = awa
She = aya
We = akhni
You (plural) = akhtun
They = ani

Possessive Pronouns
My = didi
Your (male) = didokh
Your (female) = didakh
His = dide
Her = dida
Our = deni
Your (plural) = dokhun
Their = dohun

Some examples of the use of possessive:
Leg = akla; legs = akle. "My leg" would then be "akla didi" or "akli".

Singular	Plural
akla didi or akli	akle didi or aklay
akla didokh or aklokh	akle didokh or aklaokh
akla didakh or aklakh	akle didakh or akla'akh
akla dide or akle	akle dide or akla'e
akla dida or akla	akle dida or akla'a
akla deni or akleni	akle deni or akla'eni
akla dokhun or aklokhun	akle dokhun or akle'akhun
akla dohun or aklohun	akle dohun or aklohun

Prepositions
To me = tai
To you (male) = ta'okh
To you (female) = ta'akh
To him = ta'e
To her = ta
To us = ta'eni
To you (plural) = taokhun
To them = ta'u

As an example, let's look at the verb "to give".
He gave to me. = hule tai
He gave to you. (male) = hule ta'okh
He gave to you. (female) = hule ta'akh
He gave to him. = hule ta'e
He gave to her. = hule ta
He gave to us. = hule ta'eni
He gave to you. (plural) = hule taokhun
He gave to them. = hule ta'u

Numbers
One = khda
Two = trte
Three = tlaha
Four = arba
Five = kamsha
Six = ashta
Seven = shu'a
Eight = tmanyia
Nine = acha
Ten = asra
Eleven = kadesar
Twelve = trei'asar
Thirteen = tlta'asar
Fourteen = arba'asar
Fifteen = kamsha'asar
Sixteen = ashta'asar
Seventeen = shu'a'asar
Eighteen = tmane'asar
Nineteen = acha'asar
Twenty = asri
Thirty = tlahi
Forty = arbi
Fifty = kamshi
Sixty = ashti
Seventy = shu'i
Eighty = tmani

Ninety = achi
One Hundred = ama
Two Hundred = tri amei
Three Hundred = tlaha amei
Four Hundred = arba amei (etc)
One Thousand = alpa

Days of the Week
Monday = trusheb
Tuesday = tlahusheb
Wednesday = arbusheb
Thursday = kamshusheb
Friday = arota
Saturday = shapa
Sunday = khusheba

Basic Colors
Various shades of red (including orange, pink, even brown) = smoka
Black = koma
White (including ivory, cream, off-white...) = khvara
Green (including olive, grass etc green...) = yaruka
Blue (including baby blue, lilac...) = shin
Yellow = zarda

The remaining colors are derived from these main root words. If ever in doubt, they used names of fruit or flowers in order to be more specific. For instance, if someone looked pale, they used the word "kurkmana" to describe him, as in: He went as yellow as turmeric, from "kurkum" (turmeric). In fact, when they wanted to say "yellow" they would often use the word "kurkmana" instead of zarda and it was well understood.

Human body
Head = resha
Hair = prcha
Face = mora
Forehead = gabena
Eyebrow = broya
Eyelashes = mjulke
Eye = ena
Ear = naniya
Nose = poka
Mouth = pma
Tongue = lishana
Tooth = kaka
Lip = spa
Moustache = smbele
Beard = dkna
Chin = rska
Neck = pkarta
Throat = blo'ta
Shoulder = kapana
Hand = ida
Finger = tpelka
Nail = nanuka
Chest = sadra
Stomach = kasa
Back = khasa
Bottom = shrma
Leg = akla
Knee = choka
Ankle = gozaka
Skin = glda
Blood = dma
Bone = garma

Garments
Hat = kolya, kusiya
Headdress = shada
Man's Keffiyeh = jamadiya, jamadani
Woman's Keffiyeh or Veil = poshiya
Shirt = kamisa
Jacket = chaketa
Coat = plato
Cape = abiya, charoka
Towel or Handkerchief = pishtamala
Belt = kaish
Belt Buckle = kamak
Sash = shada
Underwear = shalvala
Trousers = sharvala
Dress or Skirt = sudra
Socks = gurve
Sandals = rashke
Shoes = pla'ave

Animals
Fly = duduva
Mosquito = pishke
Wasp = debora
Bee = dabashta
Butterfly = para
Locust = kulo
Bird = uchiya
Pigeon = kotra
Crow = kala or krkasha
Rooster = dikla
Chicken = klela
Chick = uka
Ant = mruva
Louse = kalma
Lice eggs = na've
Flea = katman

Lizard = bakmaroshke
Scorpion = dupshka
Spider = dapiroshka
Roach = dusra
Mouse = akubra
Rat = jurda
Turtle = kusala
Frog = baka
Fish = masi'ya
Rabbit = kerushka
Fox = ruvi'ya
Wolf = dei'va
Dog = kalba
Cat = katuva
Donkey = kmara
Horse = susa
Mule = kodina
Cow = tavirta
Bull = tora
Calf = golka
Livestock = arba
Sheep = barana
Goat = iza
Lamb = karka
Buck (male goat) = neriya
Deer = kazala
Monkey = maimunka
Jackal = gurga
Lion = sher
Lioness = planka
Bear = harcha

Fruits and Vegetables
Herb or Grass = gla
Wheat = kte
Barley = sa're
Millet = pra'ge
White Sorghum = khrobi
Corn = dura
Rice = rza
Chickpeas = kurtma'ne
Lentils = tlokhe
Mung Beans = mashe
Beans = pasuli'e
Eggplant = banja'ne
Zucchini = kara
Radish = pela
Turnip = shal'ame
Beetroot = salke
Red Beetroot = salke smo'ke
Cucumber = ki'yira
Tomato = tamata
Pepper = pilple
Carrot = gizara
Potato = pateta
Onion = busla
Garlic = tuma
Lettuce = kase
Meatloaf = kari
Pumpkin = kara smoka
Almond = ba'iyfka
Nut = goza
Date = kazba
Seedless Date = kurma
Fig = tena
Olive = zaituna
Pomegranate = armona
Lemon = laimuna
Grapes = besi're

Sour Grapes (for cooking) = besi'rke
Vine = daliya
Apple = kabusha
Pear = kamera
Peach = khokha
Plum = khuluchka
Apricot = mjmaja
Watermelon = shmtu'a
Melon = gndora
Elongated Melon = sharoka
Carob = kshkasha
Mulberry = tu've
Cherry = goshka
Orange = prtakala
Raisins = yavishe

Kitchen Utensils
Pot = kzkhan
Plate = senika
Spoon = mlaka
Knife = skita
Fork = treikake
Ladle = trana
Pan = mak'le
Mortar and Pestle = sitta
Saj or Wok = doka
Rolling Pin (short) = garoma
Rolling Pin (long) = tiroka
Strainer = sapio
Cup = piyla
Tray = seniya
Wooden Bowl = koda
Thick Sieve (for wheat or salt) = arbala
Thin Sieve (for flour or semolina) = makhlta

Shmuel (Shamca) Baruch

Born in 1923 in Barzan, Iraqi Kurdistan, to David and Zere Baruch. In 1951, he immigrated to Israel during Operation Ezra and Nehemiah. He was a construction worker, working for Solel Boneh, who considered it a great privilege to be among the builders of Jerusalem. He died in 1997 and was buried in his beloved mountains of Jerusalem. Yehi zichro baruch.

Dina Baruch (née Zaken)

A wonderful wife and a devoted and loving mother. She was a wise and virtuous woman, highly respected and appreciated for her kind acts. Everyone went to her for a shoulder to cry on, some good advice, and words of encouragement. She educated her children to values, culture and tradition. She died too early, in 1986. Yehi zichra baruch.

Shmuel (Shamca) and his wife Dina have nine children: Esther, Isaac, Simha, Malka, Rafi, Zehava, Rachel, Dalia and Bat-sheva. They all live in Israel and all share a great love for Jerusalem - a love they inherited from their parent.

Grandfather David Baruch

Born in 1886 in Barzan, Iraqi Kurdistan. His father, Baruch Barkuna, was a fabric trader who weaved raw wool which he bought from Muslims. Just before World War I, he married Zere of the Adony family. In 1951, he immigrated to Israel during Operation Ezra and Nehemiah. In 1954, once the ma'abarot were dismantled, they moved into a one-bedroom apartment in Nachlaot, Jerusalem. Due to his advanced age, he did not secure a steady job. He kept a religious lifestyle. David lived for many years and died in Jerusalem in 1974.

Grandmother Zere Baruch (née Adony)

A wonderful woman and a loving and devoted mother who worked hard her entire life. She took employment as a maid and a washer in order to provide for her family. Zere dreamed her entire life of immigrating to Jerusalem. In 1969 she died and was buried. Yehi zichra baruch.

David and Zere had five children: Hisne, Shmuel, Sarah, Rivka and Ruhama. They had an additional five children who died of starvation and illnesses in Kurdistan.

from left to right:
sisters Hisne, Ruhama, Sarah and Rivka.

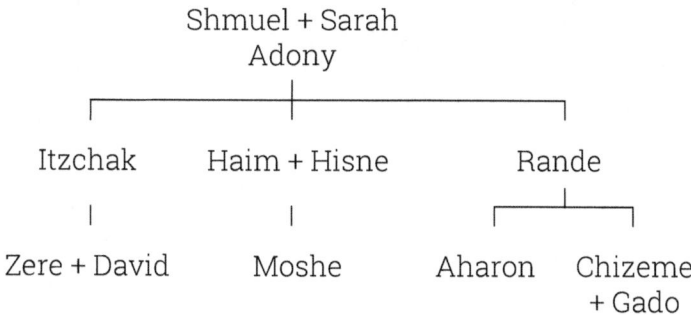

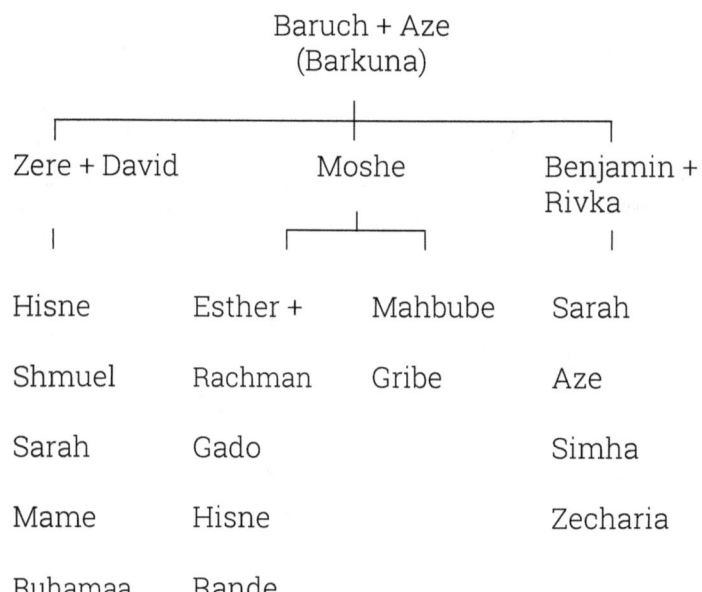

www.ingramcontent.com/pod-product-compliance
Lightning Source LLC
LaVergne TN
LVHW020927090426
835512LV00020B/3247